This Freedom

Also by Tony Parsons

This Freedom

Tony Parsons

First published in Great Britain in 2015
by Open Secret Publishing
For contact details please visit www.theopensecret.com

© Tony Parsons 2015

Cover illustration adapted from a series of paintings
Inner Landscapes by John Miller

Cover design: John Gustard

Printed by Lightning Source

A catalogue record for this book is available
from the British Library

ISBN: 978-0-9533032-4-3

With much gratitude to our dear friend, Sue Harwood, who so generously gave of her time and inspiration to help bring this book together.

CONTENTS

All there is is this . . .

the one appearing as two

nothing appearing as everything

the absolute appearing as the relative

emptiness appearing as fullness

the uncaused appearing as the caused

unicity appearing as separation

subject appearing as object

the singular appearing as plurality

the impersonal appearing as the personal

the unknown appearing as the known

It is silence sounding and stillness moving, and these words appearing as pointers to the wordless

. . . and yet nothing is happening

Preface

Apparently . . .

If someone had told me some time ago in the story that I would be talking to groups of people about a book I had written, it would have seemed unlikely and something to be avoided. However, *The Open Secret* appeared and within a short time I found myself sitting in an apartment in a London suburb about to discuss the book with five people I'd never met. As the discussion began there was a sudden recognition of a 'coming home'. It seemed as though I had arrived in a situation that expressed an inherent passion about freedom.

As a child I felt that this God I had been told about could not be much of a God if he only lived in heaven. Surely, I thought, he had to be already in everything, including me. Later when I was involved in Christianity and other teachings and processes, I never felt comfortable with the belief that there was a need for me to change, become better or be more still, more open, more focussed or whatever. The whole idea of having to make progress and become worthy of attaining some kind of higher level somehow seemed to miss the point. Was there something wrong with me, or was there another possibility?

The way in which this message emerged in such a radical and uncompromising form was at first surprising. As the contents and essence of the communication grew, then deeper and deeper layers of recognition revealed themselves. Most of the perceptions expressed thereafter would not have been originally anticipated, but clearly something had shifted or fallen away to allow for this dynamic. What also fell away was any sense of personal involvement or influence. There was no sense of ownership or any kind of held knowledge that would need to be cultivated and passed on to 'someone else'.

Thereafter I seemed to go to meetings in a kind of emptiness out of which response simply, directly and spontaneously happened without any hesitation, calculation or construction. Sometimes there would seem to be no obvious answer to a question but, as the questioner finished the last few words, a response would simply happen.

There was no question or idea here, however, that there was any channelling or sense of another source from which these responses originated. The nearest description is that this all seemed to come out of emptiness and fullness together . . . a paradox!

The other recognition that arose was that the responses were not, in any way, direct answers to a question, but more that every answer was either exposing the myth of separation or pointing to its paradox. The response seemed to originate out of no thing and return to no thing.

The essence of the open secret communication has remained constant. However there have been some words and expressions that have been discarded and the overall communication seems to be deeper and more direct.

Because this message does not originate from any kind of personal experience, knowledge or self-consciousness, then it is without agenda or purpose or motivation to fulfil a need. This makes its delivery effortless . . . it is just what is happening . . . apparently.

Another radical difference here is that as there is no presumption of there being a separate individual then there is no need or demand to change anyone or anything. The idea that the apparent seeker needs to become more still, silent, aware, detached, open, honest, or whatever else, is recognised as another illusion within the dream story of 'me'. That absence of a personal agenda can be very freeing but also very threatening. The apparent questioner may be seeking all kinds of answers and directions that can be used on what they see as a 'progressive journey'. Whatever response comes out of the open secret communication only exposes the myth of seeking or attempts to describe that which can't be known. Therefore the seeker's needs are constantly starved because the response is not really the 'answer' or guidance which is desired.

The seeker is only ever running around in circles, and the open secret's response can only go on confirming that, and illuminating the way in which it seems to happen. In the natural reality there is no real seeker, no real answer and no real time. However what can seem to happen, beyond questions and answers, is something else which is beyond words. The whole apparent contracted seeking energy sometimes seems to unravel and evaporate or collapse, but only apparently . . . and this is the paradox. There is no real contraction that needs to unravel or collapse. There is nothing real that needs to happen. There is no real seeker, path, liberation, better or worse, higher intelligence weaving a destiny and no real choice functioning at any level. All that seems to happen is only an appearance; the formless form; the relative absolute; the non-dual dualism. The no thing, not becoming the everything, but already being everything. It is the real and unreal, what is and is not. It is this real and unreal paradox which totally confounds the separate self because the self can only exist in what it experiences as real.

Because I have nothing to do with this message I am happy to say that it is very rare and in every way totally unconnected with any communication which attempts to help the seeker find something called fulfilment. There is nothing for sale and no 'you' who can or can't do anything about becoming enlightened. That idea would totally contradict the whole essence of the open secret communication.

If someone believes that they have found personal fulfilment, then they might well attempt to guide or inspire others to find the same thing. There is nothing right or wrong here . . . it is what appears to be happening. Equally there is nothing right or wrong with illuminating what is seen here as the reinforcement of an illusion. That is also what is happening . . . apparently! The open secret perception is that all seeking effort is futile because it is based on an illusory but hypnotic dream. The illumination of that dualistic dream is seen here as the only compassion, and anything else which supports that dream is a misguided effort which simply reinforces the sense of personal separation.

The term 'non-dual' is being constantly misused and has recently become a title for many teachings or practices. When I ask people what they mean by a non-dual process some seem to see it as a personal practice leading to a more fulfilling personal experience. How can this be anything other than dualism if there is someone who can choose to move to somewhere else? Surely already there are two things apparently happening. The open secret exposes what is seen as dualistic teaching.

People have asked whether this communication is happening elsewhere and of course it is, and always has been, in the story of seeking. It gets very little recognition because it is not acceptable to the dreamer in the dream story. Hidden within the communications of most major religious doctrines there is also a pointing towards the essence of what is being communicated in this message. It threatens the popular teaching of path, a process or a discipline which satisfies the seeker's need to strive in order to become worthy.

There is a very simple and direct way of recognising the fundamental difference between these two perceptions – the teaching of becoming seeks to help the seeker, the open secret does not.

The other difference is that this communication doesn't belong to anyone and is not being delivered from any kind of personal knowledge, influence or energy. There is nothing that can be transferred from anyone to anyone else because there isn't anyone.

It is sometimes suggested that the open secret message is too uncompromising. It is inevitable, however, that a message that recognises the separation as an illusory dream state can offer absolutely nothing at all to support that illusion. There are multitudes of messages or teachings that satisfy the seeker's dream for a while, but how can there be a compromise with an illusion unless it is another illusion?

Both Claire and I have watched in wonder as this message has unravelled and revealed itself to an ever increasing audience.

I knew Claire as a friend many years before a much deeper relationship happened between us. We ran a publishing business together and later on the book, *The Open Secret*, was written. It was during this period that the falling away of any sense of a separate self appeared to happen for both of us.

We had to sell the publishing business that we were running when the open secret appeared to take over our time and energy. Since that time we have worked together in organising the communication of the open secret message and we have watched it grow into how it is today.

There are so many things that I love about Claire and it seems to be so with many other people. There is, more than anything else, a welcoming gentle warmth and openness that seems to embrace those who meet her. There is also a strong sense of integrity that emanates from her and which allows people to be very open and trusting with her. She has a natural sensitivity about what is being shared, and there is a deep intuition which will quickly recognise what is going on and will also sense compromise or anything hidden. She has a wonderfully expansive sense of humour. Her easy serenity and readiness to welcome those around her is a great joy. When I watch her talking to people at meetings, but also 'out in the world' she has a way with her that seems to immediately open into a friendship in which there is a sharing and often laughter together. She has many close friends who just value being with her. There is a quality there in which people know it is safe to share anything, and also sense that it is held and nurtured.

We have close friends outside of this work but have also made many friends through this communication and this message. The support and inspiration for what is happening is tremendous. The joy and freedom of the sharing of this message has touched us both very deeply and we are always in wonder at the simplicity and directness of this communication, and how it has come about.

When there is no sense of hierarchy, of there being someone special who has something that other people don't have, then there is a natural freedom and joy that arises out of that openness.

All of yesterday's worn-out ideas, beliefs and constraints and demands about personal change or improvement simply collapse in this unbridled let go.

The other quality inherent in such a sharing is an organic humour which arises from the recognition of the endearing and vulnerable nature of the human condition. Suddenly the exposure of the myth of the apparent importance of 'my story', the significance of right and wrong and the justification of moral and ethical behaviour, simply unravels.

In the story of this earth there is a sense here of an energetic shift apparently happening in the psyche of people that has something to do with the rebellion against the old patriarchal order of established authority.

It is very obvious that, in some areas, political authority and dictatorship is losing its apparent control and influence. The same can be said for traditional religions. There seems to be a readiness to disregard traditional constraints and let go into something more liberating.

In terms of the apparent history of spiritual seeking there also seems to have been a recent coming together of Eastern and Western influences. The ephemeral and mystical energy of the East has intermingled with the more assertive cerebral and controlling influence of the West. As a consequence there seem to be the signs of the end of the need for gurus, a special someone who has a special something, a higher guidance leading to a higher level or whatever. The belief that the seeker is unworthy and needs to be more open, or still, or surrendered to a hierarchical process, seems to be losing its fascination.

It is also interesting that recent discoveries in neuroscience and physics seem to be reaching similar conclusions to those of some mystics through the apparent thousands of years of seeking. Of course these scientific conclusions are reached through individual observation and so are inevitably story-based. The unified theory scientists seek can seemingly only arise out of a unified perception.

Many people who come to the open secret meetings have invested in some kind of seeking path. When they come across a communication that starves the seeker's needs and offers no path or process, they might revert to that which they dream they can know, do and possess. However, there can be a resonance which is beyond self-seeking, and there seems to be a growing response to the unknowable, unbounded mystery of simply being.

Introduction

Apparently. . .
A long time ago it was generally believed that the Earth was
the centre of the Universe. Today it is generally believed
that the self is the centre of the human being.

These perceptions are happening in so-called evolution,
which in the story is believed to be real. But from here it is
seen as nothing making another appearance. The following
is therefore only another story which, like all manifestations,
is simultaneously both real and unreal. It is also, however,
an interesting metaphor which illuminates the way in which
the individual, the 'I', the 'self' or the 'me' has come to be
accepted as a self-autonomous entity that has a very real
and dominant influence in what is generally thought of as
'the real world story'.

Apparently, once upon a time there were no people on
the Earth. There was just earth, rock and water, the sun
shone and it rained. As life apparently evolved animals, fish
and vegetation happened. Animals ate other animals and
vegetation. Fish ate other fish and vegetation. Vegetation
just grew and it was eaten or died, and earth and rocks were

1

earth and rocks.

Things just seemed to happen for no particular reason
. . . anything that had a brain had a very simple rudimentary
brain . . . there was pain and pleasure and response and
reaction.

There was no sense of duality, right or wrong, purpose
or meaning.

However, in the story of Earth, another animal appeared
and developed a more complex and sophisticated brain. It
seems that recent research has established that the human
brain developed in such a way that part of it assumed
that the world outside of the body was a separate subject-
object reality. Consequently part of the brain constructed
a centre, or self-conscious identity, as a further investment
in its survival and a possible influence in this assumed
separate reality. The constructed self, 'me', only existed and
functioned within this subject-object dualistic reality.

Everything experienced by the 'self', the 'I', and the
'me' . . . thoughts, feelings, conditioned responses and so
on, were all apparently produced and orchestrated from the
brain, and so the added artificial self became essentially the
brain's puppet.

In the apparent story however, the individual also came
to believe that it was self-autonomous and could influence
what it saw as a very real story in a very real world. The

2

partnership between brain and self came to dominate this world, or so it seems. However, without necessarily acknowledging it, the 'self', 'me', could never seem to be entirely and constantly happy in this separate reality, regardless of all its efforts to make its story better. It is as though however much it attained in terms of wealth, power, or whatever, none of it ever seemed to be quite enough.

The hunger of the separate self is insatiable because it seems that there is something constantly missing. Even contentment or the satisfaction of desire is always a temporary or passing experience. It seems as though the evolutionary marriage of brain and self has been successful for the brain in terms of apparent dominance but a failure for the self in terms of fulfilment. But evolution seemingly has no foresight.

In time terms the duration of individuality on Earth is short-lived, but its capacity to create and destroy has been extraordinary, and it includes, more recently, its apparent capacity to self-destruct.

When we bought our house some years ago there was an old plum tree in the garden which, in the first year we were there, produced an amazing amount of fruit. It was just incredible the way it went on exploding with plums, gorgeous plums. Then, when it had finished its celebration, it suddenly died. In the story of Earth, the last hundred years has apparently produced an incredible abundance of creativity in all of the arts, sciences, psychology and technology. There is also, more recently, what seems like a frenetic energy in self-indulgence in any form. Celebrity is paramount and individual success and failure have become the dominant personal theme, together with the need to be special in whatever way possible.

Individual revolt and anger set against authority, together with a demand for more freedom, is growing. What seems to be happening in the Middle East and elsewhere expresses very well the anger and resentment that apparently arises so very powerfully for the separate individual when, despite its huge and often extreme efforts, it seems unable to achieve any kind of constant fulfilment.

The need to collect more and more information and knowledge becomes a greater and more frenetic activity. Online activity in Facebook, Twitter and other communications seems to have the capacity to create a once-removed way of belonging without intimacy.

The seeking of personal fulfilment seems to have become stronger and more introspective with the processes of self-enquiry, meditation and so on. The advent of psychology and the more recent 'New Age' movement, with personal processes becoming a dominant part, all bring together a powerful focusing on the need for the individual to become more significant and empowered. All of these personal activities seem to be moving more rapidly toward some sort of self-centred culmination.

However, the question raised here is not so much to do with the seeming capacity of the self to indulge and possibly self-destruct, but more its apparently insatiable need to delude itself and thereby avoid that which is most longed for.

The Story of Me

All there is is wholeness . . . boundless energy appearing as everything . . . the sky, trees, feelings, thoughts, whatever. It is the mystery of no thing simultaneously being everything.

There is nothing apart from the boundless everything and yet, because it is free, it can appear to be separate from itself . . . it can appear to be the story of 'me'. There is nothing right or wrong in that appearance which is wholeness apparently happening.

Contracted energy seems to arise in the human being and create a sense of separation out of which arises a unique sense of identity . . . self-consciousness. The 'me' is born and the story of 'me' seems to begin. 'Me' is the story and the story is 'me' and one cannot exist without the other. They both only appear and function in a dualistic subject object reality which is maintained through the function of awareness. Everything seems to be personally experienced as a series of events in real time happening to a real 'me'. Within that story time, journey, purpose and free will and choice seem to be real.

This sense of separation is not just an idea, a thought or a belief. It is a contracted energy embodied in the whole organism which influences every experience. As a consequence the 'me' experiences a tree, the sky, another person, a thought or a feeling, through a veil of separation. It is as though 'me' is a something and everything else is lots of other separate somethings happening to 'me'. What arises from this once-removed sense is a subtle feeling of dissatisfaction; a feeling that something is lost or hidden. For most people this sense of dissatisfaction is not that apparent, and because they believe they are individuals with free will and choice they seem motivated to try and create a successful story . . . good relationships, good health, wealth, personal power or whatever else.

However, for some there is a greater sensitivity about something that seems to be missing. This feeling generates a longing for a deeper sense of fulfilment. There can be an investigation into religion, therapy or the meaning of enlightenment. Because the 'me' has become convinced that it has the means to influence its story, it also assumes that it can find deeper fulfilment through its own choice, determination and action.

The 'me' may, for instance, go to a priest or a therapist or a teacher of enlightenment in order to find what it thinks it needs.

Often because the 'me' feels it has lost something, there can be a sense of inadequacy and so what is pursued is a teaching that satisfies the need to do something which will bring about a personal transformation and make the 'me' worthy of fulfilment. All of this activity is apparently happening within the story of 'me' which is functioning in an artificially dualistic reality. So 'me' is searching in the finite for that which is infinite. It is a something looking for another something, and what it really longs for remains unobtainable by already being everything. It is rather like trying to catch air with a butterfly net. It isn't difficult, it is wonderfully impossible. The essential futility of that searching inevitably fuels the sense of a 'me' who feels even more unworthy and separate.

However, in the seeking activity there can be experiences along the way that encourage the 'me' to search further and try harder. Personal therapy can bring a transient sense of personal balance in the story. Practices like meditation can bring a state of peace or silence. Self-enquiry can bring an apparently progressive experience of understanding and strengthened awareness. But awareness is a function that needs something apart for it to be aware of. Awareness simply feeds separation, and a state of detachment can arise and be mistaken for enlightenment. All of these states come and go within the story of 'me'.

The basis of all teaching of becoming enlightened is the idea that a change of belief or experience can lead to a personal knowing of oneness, self-realisation or of discovering your own true nature. The whole investment in a progressive path goes on feeding the story of 'me' attaining something. Even the suggestion of personal surrender or acceptance can be initially attractive and bring a satisfying state . . . for a while. There are many so-called non-dual 'teachings' which feed the story of 'me' becoming liberated.

However, the oneness that is longed for is boundless and free. It cannot be grasped or even approached. Nor is there anything that would need to be done or changed or made better than that which is already everything.

The 'me' experience can be very convincing because 'the world' it lives in seems to be dominated by lots of 'mes' in lots of stories. But the 'me' construct has no constancy. All of the 'me' story is only a dance of wholeness which is without significance or purpose.

A deep and uncompromising exposure of the artificial construct of separation and the story of 'me' can apparently loosen the constraints that keep it locked in place and reveal the way in which seeking can only reinforce the dilemma. The apparent sense of separation, however, is at its essence an energetically contracted energy which no amount of conceptual clarity will ever undo.

When there is openness to the possibility of that which is beyond self-seeking and personal experience then it seems that the apparently contracted energy can collapse into the boundless freedom which already is. And still this is only another story which attempts to point to and describe a total paradox . . . the apparent end of something that was never real . . . the story of 'me'.

All there is, is boundless freedom.

○ ○ ○

There follow here and throughout the book some questions which have been asked at various meetings.

How does the collapse happen?

There is no how. Being separate only appears to happen. It is not real. So there isn't a collapse, not in any real sense. There is only appearance and this is the mystery. It is both real and unreal. You are suggesting that there is an actual event. There doesn't need to be because everything is already whole. What seems not to be there any more is the sense that everything isn't whole.

But you mentioned the collapse?

The open secret attempts to describe a story which is about something that only appears to happen. The words describe a paradox but it doesn't make it real. I could say this is 'no thing appearing as everything', those are words. They are not 'no thing appearing as everything', they are words attempting to describe that which cannot be understood. This is pointing to something beyond comprehension . . .

So if nothing is real, what is the chair?

A chair is no thing chairing. The 'me', by looking with a sense of separation, perceives it as something solid. Actually the chair is moving particles rushing around chairing, and then the 'me' looks at it and sees and experiences it as a real separate object called a chair.

You mention there is a difference between awakening and liberation?

We are talking about the story again. In the story it can seem that the seeker is walking along and suddenly there is no seeker, and then it seems that the seeker comes out of the other side of that. It thinks that something amazing has happened and wants to be in that. That period before the collapse, or not, is what is called awakening. It is an awakening energy, a dancing between 'meing' and 'being'. This can go on for years or minutes, there aren't any rules. It is both real and unreal.

Yesterday you talked about the waves and the ocean. Is the story needed to know the ocean?

Nothing is needed. The waves and the ocean don't need each other, they are both what is and isn't. Nothing needs anything because everything is already whole. Within the whole, something arises which feels it is separate and that is when need arises. Within wholeness arises the apparent story of 'me' and 'me' believes that it needs things, has intention, thinks it has free will and thinks it can make its story better. It is no thing appearing as a separate something.

Seeking and the story is simply the absolute expression of wholeness. It is perfect already. The needing is experienced by the 'me' and is illusory. The beginning and end of it is that everything is whole but the idea that you can find that wholeness is illusory and futile. You don't need to find it because it already is that. But those are just words; energetically that is what is happening . . . apparently.

Looking for being is believing that it is lost. Has anything been lost, or is it simply that the looking obscures? Does the beloved always dance constantly just beyond our focus?

What changed in daily life after you got so-called liberated; going to work, buying the groceries . . . ?

I didn't get liberated. So nothing needed to change. Life went on as it did before but for no one. The idea that there would be a change would mean that something was better than it was before. The sense of being separate from life simply was not there anymore. You could call that a change if you wish, but actually nothing happens. What you could say is there isn't an apparent 'me' sitting on the shoulder making judgements about experience; better groceries or worse groceries. That is no longer there. Everything is harmonious in that sense; even disharmony is harmonious; it simply is what is.

The 'me' likes to think that 'isness' is also just a story.

The 'me' can only interpret things from its own perspective. It sees everything from a dualistic viewpoint.

When I hear you speaking it is such a paradox. It feels like nothing matters, it is such a love. But the mind sees this as a better story.

The seeking mind can only revert to some kind of story. It wants to continue being there, so one way is to turn this into a religion, or an idea that there is no one here, or a formula. It thinks there must be a better way, but it has to be for 'me'.

The energetic shift is what apparently happens, so does the mind recognise it?

It never can. There is no such thing as a real mind. Separation is apparently energetically held in the body but there are ideas about it as well, about 'me' being here and how it should be. Basically the energy of the construct of ideas and belief systems can never comprehend this, because the whole essence of 'me' is functioning within a finite world and it cannot comprehend the infinite.

So what you say is not important, so why do you say the mind gives up?

It isn't that the mind gives up; the illusion of separation is suddenly no more. The ideas about 'me' being something that is real, collapse with the energy. The thought that 'I am separate' is just a concept that expresses what is felt bodily. Separation has nothing to do with belief, thought or ideas; they are just a verbal confirmation of something that is energetic.

Do you think there is a purpose for you and your teaching?

No, there is no purpose and no personal teaching.

But why did you write a book and why do you come here?

I didn't write a book, I didn't come here. A book was written. That is what apparently happened.

Did it happen for a purpose?

No, that is the dream. There is no purpose; the idea that something has purpose and value is the idea that you exist. There is no you. There is only no thing, only empty fullness.

So if it is only an appearance, can anything happen?

Absolutely, anything could happen. There is no way of knowing what is going to happen next in the appearance. It is all apparent. It is no thing appearing to happen.

Is it more unpredictable when there is no one there?

It is always unpredictable. There isn't someone living in unknowing. There is only unknowing. This is new, this is no thing appearing as this. It is only 'me' that gets frustrated and thinks that everything is knowable, and therefore disappointing.

In some way emptiness can be a presence, an eternity. Is it the same thing as what we would call God?

Words like 'Presence' and 'God' can become objects to be found. This is everything. This is not an object; it remains hidden by being everything and it can't be found or known.

I was writing a prayer but my prayer seemed to be all the qualities you talk about . . . but it is still an object . . .

Some people talk about silence or stillness. But 'what is' is not silent or still, it just is. No words can describe what is. The other paradox is that words and prayers are also what is.

There are certain communicators who have not dropped their identity. Can their message, which may be their experience of nothing, be turned by our perception – so we can forgive them for our own belief in what they are saying?

There is no such thing as an experience of no thing. There is nothing to forgive. Even pure dualistic teaching comes out of no thing. When there is no one, it is recognised that there is no possibility that there is anyone else to help. The whole basis of teaching personal liberation comes from someone wanting to help someone else find something. It is based on the idea of two. Anything that seeks to help another person is dualism, which is wholeness appearing as separation, apparently.

What do you think is meant by the term 'Neo-Advaita'?

The term 'Neo-Advaita' has been adopted, it seems, by traditional Advaita teachers to portray contemporary teachings, which claim to be Advaita or Non-dual, as nothing more than superficial attempts to communicate what traditionalists see as a deeply complex set of spiritual beliefs and disciplines. The banal suggestion is that traditional 'not-twoness' is superior to new 'not-twoness'. However, despite this issue, there has apparently always been a hidden communication which is beyond the need for traditions, teachings and titles.

Is everything unfolding freshly at every instant? You said everything is new so . . .

It is only appearing to unfold. It is timeless. It is the mystery. There is no such thing as every instant.

What about faith? Unless what is real is real it requires faith.

Faith is a construct that supports dreams and hopes. People have a dream about religion; they hope and dream that it is real and that is how faith is created. It is about projecting your hopes and dreams into something that you want to have. You can't do that with this because the 'me' doesn't want this. The 'me' doesn't want absence, so you can't have faith in your own absence. 'Me' wants to continue, it is desperate to survive and will do anything it can to continue. One of the most effective ways is to seek because seeking is wonderfully futile and therefore it will continue. The worst thing for 'me' would be to become absent. Ironically 'me' chases all over the world trying to find that which is already everything.

By seeking the myth it dreams it can attain, the seeker effectively avoids that which it most fears . . . its absence.

What did you mean when you said the 'me' owns the suffering?

The 'me' is like a big sticky bun which sucks in energy. It experiences everything as happening to 'me' and being mine. It apparently makes all thoughts and feeling its own. It thinks it can become successful and also that it can become enlightened. It believes it can be personally enlightened. This is how the 'rich man' seems to appear . . . apparently.

I was in a monastery for twelve years and there was such nonsense; like ownership of unworthiness. But all games we play are like that and why don't we want to die?

Because the 'me' is fascinated by the search. All we are doing here is exposing the 'me', the 'I', the 'self', which lives in an artificial reality of its own. It dreams that it is absolutely real and everything that arises is also only real. "I am real, I live in a real story and I have real free will and choice. I live in a real story which has meaning and purpose and I can learn from other people how to make my life work. I can learn to follow a path to become enlightened." But what it longs for is the infinite, the freedom and boundlessness of the infinite which is all there is. The 'me' lives in, and only experiences, a limited, subject-object apparent finite world. If there is no finite dreamt world there is no 'me'. It can't stop being 'me' chasing something it will never find.

The function of 'me' is to seek. 'Me' is born out of separation, and the nature of separation is always to seek. The energy of separation arises and directly separation arises 'me' arises and it can only search or long for home, for oneness. We are exposing the possibility that 'me' is a dream that can collapse, and we are also sharing the realisation that there is no such thing as a 'me' or an 'I' which can find another thing called enlightenment.

Could you say more on the divine lover, and the relationship with the story and the nothingness?

There is no relationship between the divine lover and no thing. No thing is the divine lover. No thing is also everything; this is no thing appearing as everything. There

19

isn't no thing up in a cloud, in a pink absolute church in the sky delivering down the relative. What is is no thing and that is the paradox. There is no way that this can be understood or known. There is no relationship between the divine lover and no thing because they are the same. What you are sitting in is unconditional love. This is not a spiritual message, but the reality is that what is happening here is that no thing is appearing as everything. So actually everyone in this room is being made love to constantly. So an ache in the body, or feeling warm, or thinking, is the beloved. There isn't anything that isn't the beloved. That love is unconditional. It doesn't choose someone because they look nice or have been meditating for the last three weeks.

Unconditional love is boundless and it is touching everyone in this room right now through being what is happening. The mind will say, 'how can that be if there is pain or distress?' Well distress and pain are wholeness paining and distressing. You can't escape what you long for, it won't let you, it is this already. The problem for 'me' is that it thinks it is going to happen one day. Enlightenment isn't going to happen one day, it is this, already. When the artificial apparent 'me' collapses, all that is left is what is. So enlightenment isn't something happening to someone, it is the everything already.

So the lover interrupts the ego seeking?

No it doesn't interrupt it. The lover is no thing appearing as the ego seeking. Otherwise we are into dualism. There is nothing wrong with seeking. The ego and seeking are just what seems to be happening. The lover isn't interested in disrupting anything because the lover is everything, including apparent disruption.

So even though when I am here and my mind is much more settled, that is nothing to do with the beloved?

Being peaceful and not being peaceful is the beloved.

But the 'me' can't ever know this?

The lover is a magician; the free energy can travel faster than light and can appear to be separate from itself. So the beloved can appear to be separate from itself and climb up mountains and eat rice and live in caves looking for that which already is. It is absolutely meaningless. If it had meaning it wouldn't be free. What we long for is absolute freedom, but that is frightening for the 'me' because freedom cannot be controlled.

What is the experience of you standing there?

I can't tell you. What is and is not cannot be described. It is unknowable because it is the whole. If it could be described then it could be known. It is totally ordinary and natural and staggeringly obvious, to no-one.

The dropping of what was not real, what words should I use?

You can't use words because it is incomprehensible. How could something that is not real drop?

But there is an alteration or change that apparently happens?

It is wholeness simply appearing to change. The appearance of change is both real and unreal.

So nothing changes or happens?

Nothing changes and, even worse, nothing happens. This is incomprehensible to the 'me' because the 'me' lives in a world of happenings and lives in a world of knowing things are happening. It is totally illusory. There are many teachings of self-enquiry that talk about the final result being consciousness or everything knowing itself. 'Me' can't escape from the hope that in the end 'me' will find an answer. The answer must be that consciousness knows itself. It is a fairy story that comes out of the absolute and abject fear of unknowing. Unknowing is horrifying to 'me'; it means 'I will be absent' and so the teaching is that the final target is to know that I am. However, there is no I to be am.

It is not possible to understand, but is it 'me', the basket with a hole in it that wants to hear this all the time? I come every time because I want to hear this again and again. Is that the seeker or something else?

For the seeker the last thing it wants to hear is this. It thinks it wants to hear this and what is clever is that it comes and doesn't actually hear it. The seeker cannot hear that there is no one, it is utterly impossible. It doesn't matter because hearing it or not hearing it is completely irrelevant. This is beyond the words.

I come again and again and when I go home I feel more at peace. I thought it was because of what you said?

You could say that what is being said loosens something that is being held. The 'me' also collects all sorts of ideas about itself and seeking. There are so many people out there trying to teach somebody how to become enlightened, so the 'me' collects all sorts of ideas about the nature of enlightenment. To some extent what is spoken about here can loosen that and illuminate the utter futility of the idea of becoming enlightened. What else can apparently happen here is that energetically the contracted sense of there being a 'me' meets impersonal boundlessness. That constricted energy can apparently evaporate into boundlessness, into 'all there is'. It is the energy of coming home, and it is absolutely beyond words. It is a bit like light and darkness; in some way there seems to be more light and then the darkness comes back again, never quite as much as it did before and lightness seems to grow. What is said here only points to infinity and not away from it. There is nothing here telling you that you can find the infinite. That is why it is a rare message which is constantly rejected.

Can you say something about the unity of opposites?

In the natural reality there are no opposites that are real. All opposites are only an appearance. In that natural reality it is absolutely obvious to no one that everything is both real and unreal. Because there is nothing real about anything, then 'what is' has no power or significance, it is just an appearance. In the appearance there seem to be opposites, but there is nothing significant or powerful about apparent opposites. In the world there appear to be male and female opposites, but in reality they are oneness appearing as a male and female energy. They are a metaphor for liberation. The female energy is attracted to and repelled by the male energy, and vice versa. But when they apparently let go and come together there is nothing left but oneness. Apparent opposites are all an expression of wholeness. So the manifestation is totally neutral because it is no thing manifesting. It doesn't have anywhere to go or come from, it is neutral. There is no real law. It is energy appearing and being everything and no thing.

It is so obvious and simple that the grasping of it obscures it. Never found, never lost, never knowable, being is the consummate absence that is beyond measure.

Personal or Impersonal?

The titles 'Non-dual' and 'Advaita' attempt to describe the principle of wholeness, unicity or that which is already at one. During the last decade there seems to have been a growing interest in what is known as 'Advaita' or 'Non-dual' communication about enlightenment. The recent Conscious TV interviews and the beautifully crafted DVD '*Who's Driving the Dreambus*' represent a fair cross-section of people of so-called 'non-dual' persuasion but whose perceptions seem to vary considerably. There is a multitude of books published on the same subject with wildly differing views. These days the term 'non-dual' is being used for all kinds of seeking activities. You can go to non-dual conferences or indulge in a '12-month course on non-dual enlightenment'. Non-dual therapy is available, and there is even an online 'non-dual' speak club which 'no-one' can join! For anyone interested or newly investigating this subject, it can all be very confusing.

However, the open secret perception is that there are two distinctly different kinds of communication about the nature of enlightenment. One is personal and the other is impersonal. The first offers the seeking 'person' help and direction to find something called enlightenment. The second offers the 'person' nothing. The first comes in many forms and has a wide following because it seems to respond to the 'person's' needs. The second is unfamiliar and energetically confronting. The personal message is based on the belief that there is something called a separate seeker that can attain something else called enlightenment. The impersonal sees the embodied sense of seeming to be separate and unfulfilled as an illusory state which drives the apparent seeker to search for another illusion called personal enlightenment.

Any communication that supports and encourages the seeker's belief or idea that it can find something it feels it has lost is only reinforcing and perpetuating a dualistic illusion. It's not right or wrong . . . it's what apparently happens. The impersonal perception is that all concepts, ideas, beliefs or thoughts about separation or enlightenment can only ever be a reflection of their opposite, and so they are only ever pointers towards, or away from, that which cannot be expressed or known. Apparent separation is seen essentially as an embodied contracted energy which can apparently simply and suddenly release into that boundless aliveness which is unknowable and impersonal. The circumstances are totally irrelevant. No amount of clear or confused concepts can ever touch or influence that energetically held sense of being apart.

A deeply felt 'spiritual experience' can, to some people, seem to be an event of personal enlightenment. There can arise a wish to help or teach other people to have a similar experience. That communication can sometimes seem to be 'non-dual' when the teacher describes the nature of oneness, but it contradicts itself by recommending a process which can help the seeker attain that oneness through self-enquiry, meditation or purification, for example. There can be the encouragement to 'live in the moment' or 'be here now' or 'embrace the fear' in order that the person can find, 'their own true nature'. These kinds of personal prescriptions are often accompanied by a repetition of inspiring but only ever positive ideals which can lift the seeker's feelings and give them renewed hope and purpose. It seems that this kind of exchange between two people is, by its very nature, happening within the story in time, and so its influence is transitory. It fulfils a need . . . for a while.

An impersonal communication recognises and illuminates the apparent dilemma for the seeker of seeming to be imprisoned in the embodied experience of separation. It will inadequately describe the nature of unbounded aliveness and the feeling of dissatisfaction and longing that can arise out of seeming to be apart from that. It will also expose, without any kind of compromise, the absolute inevitability and hopelessness of seeking and the gift of freedom that is hidden within that hopelessness.

No-one can claim ownership of this impersonal message and so there would be no motivation to sing its praises.

Neither would there be any personal agenda to please, help or change the 'person'. There is nothing here for the 'person' except the awful possibility that everything that they dream and hope for themselves could be lost.

Whenever the personal identity, its seeking, its hopes and dreams seem threatened, there can be a rejection of this message and a return to that which seems to serve and support the uniquely human illusion of self-autonomy leading to self-fulfilment. The impersonal message can then be seen as judgemental or nihilistic and may even be felt to be 'unloving' because it leaves the 'person' with nothing. Certainly there can be something confronting about the singular constancy that arises only out of that unconditional compassion which reveals the illusion of personal imprisonment. Out of that revelation, can arise a resonance which is no-one's.

How can the 'person' hear the impersonal?

How can there be a knowing of the unknowable?

How is it possible for a 'person' to 'confront their own absence'?

How can the seeker grasp that which is already everything?

It isn't difficult . . . it's impossible . . . and wonderfully irrelevant because there is nothing separate to grasp.

Wholeness is already all there is! It is the unbounded, impersonal, unconditional freedom which is already complete . . . nothing is needed by that which is everything!

However, and this is the paradox, wholeness, being everything, can also appear as anything. . .

Wholeness can appear as the story of self on a meaningful journey.

Wholeness can appear as a separate person with free will and choice.

Wholeness can appear as a person who seems to be enlightened and helps other people to become enlightened.

Wholeness can appear as a communication which divides and calls itself non-dual.

So, in the play of appearance, wholeness can pretend to be something apart which is rushing around all over the place looking for that which already is. It is an amazing and unfulfilling dream-like story which is uniquely human and is also sublimely without purpose. For the apparent seeker, however, the pain and longing of separation seems very real.

So, should the seeker climb the spiritual mountain or simply let go and surrender to life . . . is that the question?

Or is it possible that there is no question and no answer. Maybe what is sought is all there is. Perhaps the beloved that is longed for is already constantly happening . . . it never went away . . . the seeker did, to look for it.

Perhaps, when the seeking dream dissolves into that unbounded energy, which sees no separation and has no agenda or expectation, then suddenly that longing is embraced in that unconditional love that is no-one's.

O O O

The following is an example of how the open secret meetings might be introduced:

So we are sharing a mystery together. The mystery is that all there is is the absolute relative, the formless form, the empty fullness, which is apparent energy. All there is is energy and it is utterly free. There is no thing that directs or influences energy . . . no God or Consciousness . . . energy is without intention, meaning or purpose . . . it is and is not.

Energy is also a magician. It can apparently travel faster than light and at the same time be absolute emptiness.

Energy is free and boundless and can therefore also appear as contracted apartness. When that contracted energy seems to happen in the human physiology what arises is a sense of separation . . . a sense of identity . . . A 'self', a 'me' takes apparent form and seems to be real.

30

The whole structure of self-identity is like an hypnotic dream. In the dream, as far as that self is concerned it feels it is absolutely real. "I am a real person and I live in a real world and I have a real story, the story of my life. I was born, I live and I will die and that journey has meaning and purpose".

The other thing that arises in that dream is the absolute conviction that the individual has free will and choice. It thinks it can influence its story. And the individual, in that dreamt reality, sees everything else as a separate object. So 'me', the 'I', the 'self' never sees a tree or the sky or another person as they naturally are. The 'me' sees them through a veil of separation and somehow that is unsatisfying. 'Me' lives in a dreamt reality where everything is a subject or object. "I am the subject and she, the object, is over there. The wall is there, the trees are there and I am here" and so on. The sense of separation can be deeply unsatisfying. It is maintained through awareness, self-consciousness.

There are people who are apparently open enough to recognise that there is something missing, something isn't fulfilling. Most people who live in a dream of 'me' feel in a sense they can make their lives satisfying. They subtly feel unsatisfied but they go out and maybe try to make lots of money, become powerful, have lots of lovers or whatever. They try to satisfy a hidden sense of lack. Some sensitive people feel that that lack is because of something deeper. They look for an answer in religion, or in therapy, or they might have heard of something called enlightenment and think that sounds like an answer. So they may go to a teacher of enlightenment. They have grown up believing that they are individuals and that they can, through their own choice, make their lives better. They stay within that sense of having to make an effort to find fulfilment. So they go to a teacher who will offer them personal fulfilment; a Christian fulfilment; a therapist's fulfilment where you become a more balanced person altogether; or an enlightened fulfilment where you can become personally enlightened. You are told you can attain enlightenment through following a list of instructions or whatever. That is a very powerful message. As the 'me' develops it adopts various ideas, and one of the most powerful ones is a belief in the higher and lower self. The higher self aspires and responds to any teaching of becoming which appears spiritual, and it will expend great energy in attempting to become more worthy. The teaching message is an incredibly powerful message all over the world because it speaks to the 'me' that feels lost. It speaks to the higher self. It says; "Yes, you feel lost but I can show you how not to be lost. I can show you how to become fulfilled".

So what we are sharing together is the exposure of the artificial construct of 'me', the illusory feeling that it is real and has real choice, and the awful and wonderful futility of the effort it makes to find fulfilment. We will share the illumination that the 'me' lives in a world that is finite; a subject-object world. It can only exist in that world. It exists there by being self-conscious. At a very early age self-consciousness takes over, "I am aware of myself". It grows

32

and it grows and what is sought is limited by its personal experience of that contracted reality. It seeks the infinite in an artificially finite experience that it dreams is real.

So the seeker is constantly looking from the point of view of being a subject. It is constantly looking for an object called self-fulfilment. What we are sharing together is that this whole effort is completely and utterly futile, because of the nature of 'me'. Constantly the response here will be to point to the illusory dream of there being a 'me' and to the arising of another possibility.

So we can speak together in that way but, more than anything else, the most liberating energy that is shared is unspoken. What we are really here for is about something that cannot be put into words, can't be understood, and can't be grasped. What we are talking about is a paradox. Separation is energy in an apparently contracted form. It is not a thought, belief or idea. The contracted energy that seems to be real for the 'me' can apparently collapse. What the seeker longs for has never been lost. The seeker looks for some abstract object out there but actually lives in what it longs for. So this is an exposure of an illusory dream and a pointing to something which is utterly simple and ordinary and magnificent.

O   O   O

The construct of 'me' and the apparent liberation can only happen to people, to mankind?

There is no such thing as liberation happening. The problem for the 'me' is that it is looking for something to happen. It lives in a world of what will happen to 'me' next. Liberation doesn't happen. There is no such thing as liberation because everything is already whole. All that you could say is that what apparently collapses within that is wholeness pretending to be separate. Separation is the only illusion. There is no such thing as real individuality. In this room there are only bodies, some of which feel as though they are separate people. Animals do not have the ability to abstract a sense of individual identity. Directly there is a sense of being separate from the whole, then there is seeking and living in a subject-object reality and a state of continual expectation.

Each day I feel there is 'me' but there are moments when that feeling is not there, there is just doing what I am doing. Then there are situations when there is no 'me' but awareness of things like thoughts appearing and a wide focus?

When the illusion of 'me' is no more, everything goes on as it did before but for no one.

When the illusion comes back, however, it seems so real. The next moment there is no such thing?

34

That is the state of being in limbo, 'me' and 'not me'. Suddenly there is no 'me'; it is as if something falls off that was never there.

So basically we should just get on with it?

Who is going to get on with it? That is another choice. You could also say we might as well not get on with it. You are back in the idea that you can accept it is hopeless and just get on with your life. It is absolutely hopeless for 'me'. You can't get over this sense of separation with an idea about acceptance. One of the confusions that can arise for 'me' is the idea that there is a way of being 'non-dual', like 'being in the moment', or 'being totally unidentified' or whatever. People even try hard to be 'no me'. It is a futility born out of trying to understand 'it' and then doing 'it'.

What do you think we are here at this meeting for then?

No thing. You come here thinking you might get something and it is possible that you might leave with no thing. As far as the seeker is concerned this message is completely and utterly useless. There is nothing on offer here at all.

There is no answer to life because life is its own answer. It is happening already. It is this. It was never lost. When liberation apparently happens people say, "It is amazing because the thing I was looking for has never left. It's the one thing that never comes and goes, the one constant that can't be known or held onto".

Maybe there is something to lose, although there is nothing to get. That feels good.

There is a killer in the room. The whole room is inviting 'you' to die. Everything in life, feeling warm, thinking, sitting on a seat, is an invitation to die. You live in the constant presence of that which you long for. Everything that you long for is absolutely shouting at you but it can't be heard because 'me' doesn't want to die. Knowing somewhere that it will never find what it is looking for the 'me' apparently goes on seeking in order to continue. The most effective way for it not to die is to seek.

Is there life after death?

There isn't a death. No one is born, no one lives and nobody dies. The apparent death is the end of the functioning of the dream of 'me'. That can happen in the living body or at physical death. I can't tell you what this is like, no one can. It can't be known. The end of 'me' is unknowing, so no one can tell you. But the mind will always reject this, and many teachings in the world will tell you how you can deal with the prison of the 'me'. This is because of belief in the fantasy of a 'me'. Any personal teaching feeds dualism by believing it can find an answer. There isn't an answer because there isn't a question.

I believed I had all that; I believed I had had an awakening and made a website, but now I am back where I started.

36

What is wonderful is that you haven't started. There is no one to start and nowhere to go to.

So is there no sense to life?

It depends what you mean by life. There is life appearing, but that appearance is completely without meaning or purpose. If there was a purpose there would be a journey, or a tomorrow. That is the 'me' dilemma. There is only the infinite; you are looking at the infinite. It doesn't need a purpose, it is already complete and fulfilled. The sense of life is full on.

I had teachers before and they believed that what they said was true – so the 'me' is capable of producing this?

The 'me' is apparently hugely powerful in its meaningful story. Often when people feel they are personally fulfilled and become teachers that produces a huge power for other people in the story. If people walk into a room when the teacher is in the dream of self-empowerment, they feel something. But it is all emotional, a game of experiences. It seems powerful and is completely meaningless. There are a lot of so-called non-dual teachings which are very eloquent about oneness but then tell you what to do to find it. There is only oneness. How can one be two that can find one?

What can seem to happen is that there can be a dis-identification with the conceptual sense of self, together with a transient experience or awareness of a state of 'presence without concepts'. However this is still a subject-object dichotomy which can sporadically identify with this state of 'presence'. There can be a sincere attempt to teach other people how to 'reach' that same experience, but it is all still happening in the dream story and is therefore a transient state.

Recently some teachers have claimed that they have experienced non-dualism and moved on to something greater. What is that all about?

It is all about the incomprehension of the nature of non-dualism. There seems to be a common and false idea that non-dualism is a personal state of 'living in the moment', or 'knowing there is no me', or 'finding your own true nature'. Non-dualism is a term, like Advaita, which refers to the mystery of oneness and no thing being everything. It is not a personal experience that can be turned on and off. The claim that someone can experience nothing being everything and then move onto something greater is ludicrous. It usually comes out of incomprehension or the need to be special.

Sometimes the words are similar to here but the opposite happens. Does the 'me' sense the danger of disappearing so it produces something like it in order to stay? Sometimes the words are for learning about this.

This is not a personal teaching, this is an illumination.

There is no attempt to help anyone because it is recognised that there is no one to help. There cannot be an agenda, or anything to help. However there are quite a few teachings that use a similar language which only come out of a conceptual understanding usually undermined by dualistic proposals. Anyway, it is only wholeness pretending to be a teacher trying to help wholeness pretending to be a student.

Different people have different wording, and something else was transmitted which settled the sense of needing to improve me.

It is clear that teachings help people to feel better and that is called compassion. Actually it is the opposite because it is reinforcing and supporting the prison. They just make the prison more comfortable . . . for a while. It is a complicity to continue with the dream.

Does that mean that psychiatrists and psychotherapists just do this? After liberation how could they function?

The only thing that could happen with people who work with others is that their work would apparently change and they would start to introduce this illumination into their therapy. They would then attract those people open to that possibility. Although it is not the 'me' that is open, when there is an opening to that and it meets no thing pointing to something beyond the self, that's where liberation can happen . . . apparently.

So all these people who work like this, such as me, what should we do?

There is nothing wrong with it – it is just what is happening in the story. You are not a psychotherapist, there is no such thing. It is just what is happening in the story; the whole manifestation is a story. The infinite doesn't become the finite, the absolute doesn't become the relative, they are both the same thing. There is only the absolute relative and the infinite finite. They can seem to be separate to the 'me' which thinks it is real. But it is the formless forming; they are both simultaneously happening.

So there is energy. How does that body which can be called Tony Parsons relate to anger or emotions?

Everything is energy. The end of 'me' is the end of apparent relationship. Relationship is about one and another. So there is only anger. The body can have the energy of anger in it. All there is is what is, anger. It is real and unreal and only apparently there.

You haven't always been like this. When Tony Parsons changed, did you know there was only zero?

Tony Parsons apparently died. This doesn't know anything. This comes straight out of no thing. It is the one thing that can't be known or described.

Did it happen in one time or is it a process?

It never happened. When there is a seeker there can be an apparent dancing in 'meing' and 'being' and then apparent liberation seems to happen. There is nothing left. All there is is what is and isn't. Liberation doesn't happen.

While listening to you, the mind tries to grasp the whole thing and draw some conclusions. The 'me' is trying to get something.

The mind is trying to get something to live by, or an understanding. The seeker tiptoes around the edge of the infinite looking for a way in. It is trying to find, in the finite, what it can relate to that is infinite. This message is not living in some absolute existence, it is constantly pointing to aliveness in sitting on a seat, breathing, hearing noise, thinking. What is, is inescapable. Even if you reject the idea, that is also what is. All there is in this room is what is. It can't be escaped from. It is the perfect lover and the grim reaper. It will never let you go until you fall into its arms.

Why are there teachers of impersonal and teachers of personal messages?

There is no real person, no teacher. But the communication either comes out of the personal or impersonal. So all the time it is coming out of the personal it is offering personal guidance, a path to somewhere else. That comes out of an energy that is still in the story. Something personal feels as if it has got something to help other people find liberation. As far as the open secret is concerned, that is still in the illusory story. It is rare for the impersonal message to be communicated, but it always has been available because there has always been a readiness to go beyond the person. The personal message, to do with somebody learning something to get somewhere, is the most popular. This is not a criticism but it is a way of trying to explain the absolute difference between those two messages. There is no meeting at all between that which comes out of no thing and that which is offering something to an apparent someone.

The unified reality in which there are 'not two', or there is 'no thing apart', surely confirms the illusory nature of separation. If separation is illusory, then any attempt not to be separate is rooted in a dualistic perspective. So the basic principle of any teaching which attempts to transform an illusory state of being separate into a state of at-oneness is based on the belief in a divided reality and cannot therefore claim to be non-dual.

Time is a concept of me?

For the 'me' time is real. It may give lip service to there being no time but 'me' feels it is real. "I was born, live and will die". In the natural reality time is both real and unreal. Everything is both real and unreal. Energy is completely wild and free. It may appear that there will be 6pm tonight but there may not be. Nothing is predictable and no one knows what will happen next. You cannot predict that time is a constant. Everything is new after liberation. It is indescribable. It wasn't there before and it won't be there tomorrow. The 'me' dreams it lives in a predictable known world; "I saw the floor yesterday and I now know it". Then suddenly that apparently known reality collapses. So it is a constant love affair, but nobody is in it. There is just being-ness that is totally alive and just is. It is knowing or being aware of it that turns it into something that is artificially lifeless. Knowing it takes the life out of it, and then you are safe for a while.

I get confused. How can we come to the natural reality?

The 'me' lives in an artificial reality apparently in time. 'Me' cannot come to that which already is. There is only wholeness which is completely free to appear as a contracted ○ energy. The contracted energy seems to arise as an apparent identity which lives in a dualistic reality. All that is going on here is a description of the way 'me' seems to experience it. There is no such thing in reality but the apparent 'me' seems to experience a dualistic reality through the function of awareness.

I hang on the words only.

If you can only hear what the words are literally saying, then you are stuck in avoidance. They are only pointing to something. A lot of people don't listen to anything here and that is fine. It is not about only listening to the words.

After liberation, is there still a personality and habits?

It depends what you mean by personality. The persona is a sort of mask which the 'me' wears in order to 'make it' in the world. The 'me' apparently takes on roles to make its life work and one is a mask or presentation of how it would like people to see it. After liberation, all sorts of things collapse including the mask and self-consciousness. There is no agenda or wish to please and there is no sense of any free will and choice. There is no self to be conscious. There is no longer any sense of there being anything here or anything out there looking at this. There aren't relationships anymore; there is nothing to relate to. There is obviously interplay of energies but there is not anyone who is in them. Preferences can arise and the body organism has characteristics and preferences like music or marmalade, but that is only energy playing and doesn't need a 'me' for it to be.

What is fulfilment?

Even that word doesn't really say this. There is no way of describing what is there after – except what is and isn't. Before liberation there is a longing for fulfilment, 'me' is seeking something it doesn't understand. There are no words.

There seems to be relief and there seems to be less and less holding on.

'Me' might be in less holding on for the rest of its life. This is about the end of 'me', the illusion of separation.

The fish in the fishbowl feels thirsty, looking for water . . .

The problem for the 'me' is that it is looking for an object, ○ something to hold onto. What it doesn't realise is that it is living in that which it longs for. It is all there is. The 'me' can't get this because it lives in a subject-object world.

The open secret communication can only point to the simple wonder of being and attempt to illuminate the futility of seeking for it. It does not accept or reject the teachings of spiritual path or process but it will expose, without compromise, the singular and fundamental illusion that drives the belief that there is something called a seeker that is able to find something else called enlightenment.

It seems that love and hate are an appearance so there is no polarity or distinction between right and wrong. But at the same time there are choices to be compassionate and kind rather than killing?

Everything that arises here is out of nothing. There is no controlling, and it arises out of no thing, that is all there is. 'Me' lives in the dream world that thinks it chooses compassion over killing. In the natural reality there is just a spontaneous response and you can't say it has anything to do with goodness or badness.

You said about seeing the futility in what 'me' is doing. In the process of trying and trying there was exhaustion. There was a collapse of the whole system. So because I am not investing in those kinds of things, the seeking is still happening and is investing back in materialistic things. Only recently I've seen that the futility that is around spiritual practices is around materialism. You could make a million pounds but you can't buy this moment. So it is all worthless, what is the point?

Spiritual practices are materialistic; it is something for you. There is nothing wrong with making a million pounds or those spiritual practices. They just make things more comfortable. But they don't last. They come and go. The one thing that doesn't come and go is what is and is not; it is all there is.

Sometimes people have spiritual experiences, then they do the seeking. We have enlightened masters in China who tell us about enlightenment.

The 'me' believes that by doing something it can gain enlightenment, but that is a complete myth. There is no such thing as an enlightened person. There is no person to become enlightened. Trying to find spiritual enlightenment is like trying to lift yourself up by the armpits. The 'me' is only self-seeking.

So what is really going on here with this seeking?

The whole energy of 'me' is trying to gather in these thoughts and ideas. Underneath that is its impulse to be one again. But it doesn't want that because it would lead to the end of 'me'. So it feeds itself with spiritual, mental and physical things. Here, you have come to an empty shop. You are here because you think you might get something . . . but you might leave with nothing.

It feels as if it is self-evident, but there is still longing.

'Me' longs for freedom from the prison, but it longs for something it doesn't comprehend. You are longing for that which already is; it never left you, it constantly is, it never went away.

When I see this is all there is, I say, is this really all there is? It is disappointing.

It is 'you' that makes it disappointing! All there is cannot be seen. What keeps the beloved apart is your awareness. Because you are aware of what is happening you keep it apart. Sitting on the seat is the beloved. It is no thing arising as sitting on a seat. The 'me' keeps it apart because it dreams that it knows that 'me' is sitting on a seat, and by apparently knowing, it is constantly disappointed.

"The kingdom of heaven is like a mustard seed." It is ordinary, it is just this, and it is immeasurable freedom.

What about love, compassion and grace – don't they help?

There is nothing that needs help. This is already what is. If there was a need for help there would be somewhere to go and something to do.

I was told I was not living my life because I was not aware and not doing certain things.

It is a good illusion. There is no one that can do that and the whole idea of that is complicity. It is a way of reinforcing the identity, of there being someone who should have an awareness of a life.

When the film of Tony Parsons was running did you have the feeling of awareness?

All the time there was an apparent Tony Parsons, there was awareness. Awareness is the fuel of separation. When the film dropped out and there was just light, there was no awareness. That was the apparent end of separation. Awareness is that which helps to construct a subject-object world. It is the accomplice of separation. A subject is aware of an object.

So what replaces awareness?

Nothing, because it is the fuel of the illusion of separation. Teachers claim that 'I' is certainly present because if 'I' was not present there wouldn't be awareness of these words. This is a wonderful example of the false assumption that 'I' makes; firstly that it is entirely real, and secondly that only through its awareness can anything exist. This certainty cannot allow for any other possibility. In the meantime the brain has already assimilated these words long before the apparent 'I' takes delivery of them. The 'I' then proudly announces to the world, that, through its awareness, the words have come into being. For 'I' there has to be ownership of everything and this is how 'I', the higher self, becomes a 'rich man'.

How do you see the difference between awakeness and awareness?

There is no connection. If you call awakeness 'what is', then there is nothing in it that needs to be aware.

But there is a perception of 'what is'?

No, there is just 'what is'. When there is no longer an illusion that there is something separate all that is left is 'what is'. There is no perceiver that is real.

But surely when 'me' asks a question here there is an awareness of it over there and then a response?

When 'me' asks a question it is aware of that questioning

49

and of the response arising within its own subject-object reality. However, in the natural reality, both the question and the response are simply something apparently happening out of no thing. There is no awareness and no here or there that is real.

So everything is happening in free-fall?

Apparently.

Is there consciousness?

Consciousness, knowing and awareness are similar apparent functions within wholeness. Awareness is the function through which the apparently contracted energy of a separate identity arises. The function of awareness re-establishes and maintains the illusory sense of a self . . . self-awareness . . . consciousness of self . . . self-consciousness!

The apparent self, or 'me', can only exist through awareness which sustains a subject-object reality, i.e 'me' (the subject) is aware of sitting on a chair (the object). It is the content of the great hypnotic dream that is assumed to be the 'normal reality'.

When the illusion of the separate 'me' collapses, personal awareness, knowing and consciousness collapse also. Of course functioning appears to happen, but happily without the already redundant constrictions and judgements of the 'me' which was never ever needed to cook a risotto, drive a

*just carrying
me contracted
energy for the ride*

car, write a symphony, or analyse a protein.

But surely the no thing that is and isn't, knows itself?

It doesn't need to know it is and is not. It is an illusion that consciousness knows consciousness, or no thing needs to know that it is everything. No thing doesn't need to know anything, because it already is everything. Why would it need to know that? Where would it go to stand apart and know itself?

I am not talking about a consciousness that is apart, I am talking about a consciousness that is in it.

So consciousness is another word for knowing or awareness, and these are all transient functions . . . they are in movement. They are actions that apparently happen within wholeness. Consciousness of a tree, consciousness of self, knowing the sky, knowing I am, awareness of a thought; it is wholeness appearing to be a separate knower.

Self-enquiry is based on the limitation of personal experience. The ultimate goal of self-enquiry is variously described as 'consciousness of self'; 'awareness of the whole'; or 'knowing the known'. All of these states are only an appearance within the infinite. They are no thing appearing as the function of an apparent something knowing another apparent something. It is another story within oneness. It is the one appearing as two and awareness divides in order for 'me' to survive. The 'me', the 'self', or the 'I' will

51

apparently devise any means it can to avoid what it most fears, its absence. The teaching and process of awareness, or knowing, is very attractive to 'me' and very effective . . . for a while. A powerful but still personal experience that can arise out of this kind of introspective activity is what is often called 'self-realisation'. It happened when I was a seeker and it gave me a sense of being powerful and detached, all-seeing, all-knowing. Of course it didn't last because it was only another function within the story.

And so here we go again with another avoidance, as with all teachings of becoming, with a functional devised state that seems obtainable but is always inevitably transient and once removed: 'being in the moment' or 'knowing your own true nature'; or 'surrendering to what is'. Even the ultimate goal of self-enquiry i.e 'knowing the known', is still a subtle movement . . . a story of one and another. It is all the 'higher self' never quite being it, simply because there is no it to be.

So as consciousness is an inconstant function within the everything, how can it be the everything? Why would everything need to know that it is everything and where would it go to know that? How can there be consciousness of no thing?

Because the apparent self can only exist through its own knowing, its search for a deeper meaning will be limited to that which it can know and experience for itself. The separate seeker pursues everything that it can know and do, excepting the

absence of itself. That absence is the emptiness which is unknowable, but paradoxically it is also the very fullness, the wholeness that is longed for.

But then how does functioning happen in that location?

When something is apparently happening the brain assimilates and responds regardless of an apparent 'me' or no 'me'. This functioning is simply the appearance out of no thing. It is something that seems to be moving in time apparently doing something.

Is this complete nihilism then?

No it isn't. Nihilism is a viewpoint or belief about the existence of the world and what meaning it has. This goes totally beyond any sort of belief or denial and describes everything as real and unreal. It is beyond any idea that there is any meaning. Nihilism suggests that there is no hope and that there is no God. This is pointing to something completely beyond that. Nihilism is a philosophy, this is not.

It points to something beyond that which is life?

It points to life as it is, and isn't.

Knowing and Unknowing

The story of Adam and Eve is an allegory describing the loss of 'paradise' through the arising of self-knowing. So, it seems, there is wholeness (paradise) and within that boundless, free-floating, causeless energy, something appears which knows itself as being separate from that wholeness (paradise).

Here is a metaphor pointing to what seems like 'the story' of self-consciousness, out of which is apparently born the awareness, knowing and experience of free will, choice, time and space, purpose and direction.

As 'the story' unfolds, so the apparent self learns to know 'the world out there' and attempts to negotiate the best story possible for itself . . . it apparently takes action to find pleasure and avoid pain. The greater the knowledge the more effective the action, the results and the apparent sense of personal control . . . or so it seems.

All of these efforts bring varying results, and so the

individual comes to know fluctuating states of gratification and disappointment. However, it can be noticed that there seems to be an underlying sense of dissatisfaction which drives the self to discover and know more and more.

Because the apparent self can only arise through its personal experience, knowing or self-awareness, its search for a deeper meaning will be limited to that which it can know and experience for itself. Within these limitations there are a multitude of doctrines, therapies, ideologies, spiritual teachings and belief systems that the seeker can come to know. There can also be the knowing and experiencing of states of silence, stillness, bliss, awareness and detachment, all of which seem to come and go like night and day.

All of these teachings, recommendations and prescriptions are attempting to provide the seeker with answers to that which is unknowable, and ways to find that which has never been lost.

So the self is the separate seeker that pursues everything that it thinks it can know and do, excepting the absence of itself. That absence is the emptiness which is unknowable, but paradoxically is also the very fullness, the wholeness (paradise) that is longed for.

Should the apparent seeker meet with a communication which reveals in great depth the real nature of separation and also exposes, without compromise, the sublime futility of seeking, there can be a collapse of the construct of the separate self. That totally impersonal message carries with it a boundless energy into which the seemingly contracted energy of self unravels. A resonance can arise which is beyond self-awareness . . . something ineffable can be sensed . . . a fragrance and an opening to the wonder of unknowing can emerge.

Suddenly, there seems to be a shift and an impersonal realisation that this is already wholeness. The boundless, naked, innocent, free-floating and wonderful simplicity of beingness is already all there is . . . it is extraordinary in its ordinariness and yet it cannot be experienced, described or known.

O   O   O

What is it like to be a baby before separation . . . and is the grim reaper the ultimate redeemer?

Wholeness cannot be described. Separation is apparently brought about by the sudden contraction which brings with it an awareness of someone else entering the wholeness, usually the father or the mother. Directly there is an awareness of someone, there is a sudden self-awareness. "There is something else and I am something, I am a person". 'Me' feels it is real and that everything else is real. The sense of separation is somehow unfulfilling. Death in the body or before death is the end of the illusion, the end of separation . . . apparently.

*Will the separation happen to everyone . . . is there anything
a mother can do to avoid it?*

Separation is an illusion . . . it is not a real happening. Most
people are living in that separate illusion but it is not right or
wrong, it is like another reality. The 'me' lives in a subject-
object dualistic reality. It is artificial but most people
believe it is real and that they can do something about
their story. It's what happens to human beings uniquely;
nothing else, so far, has the capability to abstract a sense
of having a separate identity. There is nothing that can be
done to avoid it and there is no need to avoid it, it is simply
an expression of wholeness. All there is is wholeness. The
infinite chases itself all over the world looking for itself; it
builds churches and goes on crusades, and does all sorts
of things to try to find a something called the infinite. It
will never find the infinite because it can only know, in
that appearance, a separate subject-object reality. It can't
find what it is looking for because what it is looking for is
already everything.

The problem for the seeker is that they are very attracted
by the idea that they have to become worthy, so they are
attracted to teachers who tell them that if they meditate or
be open, they will become worthy of fulfilment.

So everything becomes nothing?

Everything doesn't become no thing, it already is no thing.
No thing and everything are one. So what apparently is

happening here is no thing appearing to happen. It has no purpose or meaning. It just is what it is and isn't and is both real and unreal.

You can describe it as utterly chaotic . . . is there any pre-destination?

You could say that this appearance is both ordered and chaotic. There is no predestination. If there was there would be something destined or planned. There is nothing planned because there is no future, there is no past, there is only this. All there is is 'isness', it is not going anywhere. It can't be known and the problem for the seeker is that they are looking for something to know, like peace, silence, presence, awareness or detachment. It thinks it can know that thing and have it and own it. But that is the dilemma, as it can never know this, or be this, or control this.

Does there need to be surrender?

No, there is no one who surrenders. There is either a 'me' or there isn't a 'me'. 'Me' is separation, 'me' is the seeking. There isn't anything that surrenders into not being 'me'. Surrender or acceptance are part of the story.

So there is nothing to be done – like to go to your residential or read your books?

No, it is not that there is nothing to be done; it is that there is 'no one'. The doing that seems to happen is completely and utterly meaningless. If you come to a residential you don't get any help at all. If you think you have been helped it is your belief. There is nothing here that is trying to help anyone because there is no recognition that there is anyone. All words are dualistic, but if you listen to what is said here, the words point to what is, that which is beyond the 'me'. They never point to the idea that 'me' can find it. What is going on here is a deconstruction. There is no such thing as liberation, or a seeker, it is only an appearance. We are attempting to describe something that can't be known. In the story the apparent contracted energy suddenly vanishes or evaporates back into what is. Apparent liberation is an apparent release of contracted energy back into apparent boundlessness.

The open secret's apparent communication is paradoxical, unreasonable, unbelievable, non-prescriptive, non-spiritual and uncompromising. There is no agenda or intention to help or change apparent individuality. It is prior to all teaching and its resonance is shared energetically, not through the exchange of ideas.

So anything I think has no influence on it?

Nothing at all has any influence. Already this is complete. Why would wholeness want to change that?

Would there be any fear?

There can be a tremendous fear when the 'me' realises what is apparently happening.

So should the seeker stop seeking?

This is not a message about seeking or not seeking. The 'me' energy can only seek and try to come back home. That is all it can do. When it thinks it has lost wholeness all it can do is to try and find wholeness. People believe that if they reach the pinnacle of purity, which is just a mind creation, they will then be worthy of freedom. That is the problem the 'me' has. It loves the idea of becoming pure, because it believes it is unworthy. The whole teaching of becoming is based on a fallacy that the 'me' needs to change, whereas 'me' is just wholeness appearing to be 'me'. It is meaningless and without purpose.

Can you say more on the separation and awareness, and meditation?

Awareness is the accomplice of separation. Awareness is a function which requires something for it to be aware of. When awareness arises there is a subject aware of an object. That is awareness. It is a fallacy that you should become more aware. The whole construct of self-enquiry reinforces separation. It is generally acknowledged that trying to stay in a focused awareness or knowing is impossible, and that is because these are all functional states that, by their very nature, are transient. Failing to stay in focused awareness reinforces the sense of unworthiness.

Meditation is a slightly different construct; it is still trying to get something. All that is being suggested here is that there is no one and nothing to do; there is no path.

I am where I am and it is limited and not the truth – so what is the next step?

There isn't a next step. If there is a sense of 'you are where you are' that is what is happening. That is the way it is. There isn't a truth. The idea that you are there limits that 'me' in the experience of being separate. What is being suggested here is that there is no 'real me' and no 'real' limitation.

But there is experience in this locality and not in that locality.

But that is your experience. The problem for the 'me' is that it experiences, and apparently knows and is aware that it exists. It believes that it is real and that is the dilemma. There is nothing that can let go of it and there is no 'real' location.

Is the deconstruction also unknowable?

Yes, because it doesn't happen. There is no real 'me' to vanish. So-called liberation is the apparent end of something that was never happening. You aren't happening, you feel you are. What is being suggested is that that is an illusion. All the time 'me' is trying to deconstruct 'me' it is just strengthening the illusion. Its energy is to find something and to move forward. What the 'me' is looking for when it tries to deconstruct itself is an object called 'no-me'. 'Me' is trying to investigate 'me' all the time, so that it cannot be 'me'. It gets stronger and stronger trying not to be 'me' . . . apparently.

Are you saying that this is all magic? What is it?

No, I am saying it is what is. It can't be known. What you long for is unknowing and what you fear most is unknowing. What you long for most and fear most is the absence of yourself.

But there is something else that also wants to do it.

There is a higher self and a lower self. The higher self wants to be pure and perfect, and the lower self wants to lie in bed and drink gin! Both constructs are equally illusory. All processes and teaching appeal to the higher me and speak to it; you can be still, aware, detached, and pure. It is all an attempt to attain something. There is nothing to attain. You don't need to attain this because it 'is' already. You have been rushing around looking for it but it has been there all the time.

This message has been misunderstood if it is believed that it is saying that there is a 'you' who can or can't do anything about becoming enlightened.

Is it a change of perspective?

No, it is the end of something that was never really happening. What has ended is the illusion that there is someone. That which held the sense of separation just evaporates. There is just what is and isn't?

Now, whenever I do anything wrong, I say, "well that is just the story" and there seems to be less contraction about doing something wrong.

The 'me' only dreams it can do something right or wrong. It is only another state. Like meditation, people say, "When I meditate I am peaceful". It is only a passing state.

Maybe I will be in a dream state for the rest of my life. I understand that there is only a story but I don't know it.

You don't know anything. You don't know how long you are going to live. You cannot presume anything and understanding is not liberation. It is only something else the 'me' can have. Understanding that there is no story is just 'understanding'. Tony Parsons was never real. The 'me' lives in a story about something happening; "I am going to have a cup of tea and then I am going to be enlightened", or "I have heard that Tony Parsons is enlightened so why doesn't it happen to me". We are talking in two different realities; one where the story is happening and the other where there is no story. We are talking about a mystery. There was no Tony Parsons to die, that is the illusion. Tony

The story of me
& how I should be
- based on limited experience
& it's/known
What of all else

& told d
Jeff Foster

moving

64

beyond
the isolated thno
/ known

there isn't
a set way to
conform to
Remember the
week in textbar
- no fixed me -
and all went on
- feel I became self conscious
again

Parsons thought he was real and went around trying to find real enlightenment. Tony Parsons sensed that teachings of becoming and processes were not it, but that was only a sense until there was the apparent collapse.

What can you say about unconditional love and compassion?

Unconditional love is like boundless energy and the idea that there is a quality there to describe is misconceived. Like compassion, you can't describe it. You can't describe or influence boundless energy or unconditional love or compassion. They are what is and isn't.

But there is chaos and crime . . . ?

Unconditional love is the appearance of chaos and crime, and marshmallows and Beethoven's fifth. It is everything outpouring. Someone said this morning that the 'me' is like a taking in, a grasping. The boundlessness is like a giving out, a continual flowing out. It continually gives; it is just exploding in every way, apparently.

Is this synchronicity? I could be going to a party and then deciding at the last minute to go somewhere else instead where I hear about the open secret.

Synchronicity happens in the story; synchronicity is between apparent events in the story. The story is meaningless. The synchronicity seems to lead to something of value to the person in the story but actually it is meaningless. There is nothing leading to anywhere because there is nothing going anywhere because already everything is fulfilled. As far as 'me' is concerned everything is certainly not fulfilled, and that is the feeling of being separate. When that collapses it is absolutely obvious that there is nothing that needs to be synchronised.

I thought that compassion is similar. You say true compassion is for people to be liberated?

Compassion illuminates that which imprisons the apparent self. There isn't something out there turning it on and off, it just naturally comes out of no thing. No thing naturally responds to a question, or sense of separation. People say this message is not compassionate. Helping people to become liberated is not compassion, it is complicity in the agreement to maintain an illusion . . . apparently.

Isn't it curious that the energy is wrapped up in 'me' and yet the same energy is working on it to try to undo this knot?

Energy is everything – compassion and complicity. However, energy is completely without any intention at all. The only thing that has intention is 'me' in the story. Boundless energy has no intention because it is already fulfilled. There is no knot to undo.

When you use the word 'exposes', that suggests a certain direction?

What apparently happens is that when there is something that feels it is in separation there is a response out of no thing which exposes that. There is no agenda, but that is the natural response of unconditional love. There is no expectation for something to happen because there is simply no thing appearing to happen.

But it has to work the other way as well. When there is wild energy, energy without pattern, then the response might be the 'me'?

It only appears to work the other way but strangely without any intention. This message doesn't have any intention; it just is a response, an appearance. Although it may seem to have the intention to expose, there is simply exposure. That is the paradox which cannot be explained or comprehended.

While this happens, we are wonderfully hopeless. When I leave here tomorrow there is nothing I can do?

This message illuminates the helplessness and the dilemma of the 'me'. It exposes that 'me' is an illusion or a dream. You won't leave here tomorrow. You will only appear, or you will dream, that you are leaving here.

So this apparent story of 'me', can you equate that with a dream we have at night?

Yes, it is the same thing. When 'me' wakes up it dreams it has stopped dreaming.

So liberation is a gentle or rough awakening from that dream?

It doesn't matter, but it is an apparent awakening from an apparent dream. No one is dreaming, but the 'me' is the dreamer. For the 'me' the dream is that I am real, my story is real and also my influence on that story.

But nothing wakes up from the dream?

No, nothing wakes up . . .

The way we use words, we use them and apply them within the dream of the 'me', to something that is impersonal, that has no direction and no intention.

Yes, and we are conditioned to believe that certain words mean certain things. Like Jesus using the word 'repentance'. I went to a Catholic school and I was taught that you should be sorry for a sin and seek repentance. Maurice Nicoll said in one of his books that the word used at the time Christ was alive meant 'turning around and seeing life anew' . . . completely different. That was an amazing revelation in my life as a seeker.

As we move from one formula to another, we seem unable to see that freedom does not reside here or there, simply because freedom, by its very nature, cannot be excluded or exclusive. We seem not to see that, as we march towards the next anticipated

spiritual high, the treasure that we seek is to be discovered, not in where we are going, but within the simple nature of the very footsteps that we take.

I keep being tempted by the idea that when I leave here it is going to be different. At the end of the day it is all based on the illusion of the apparent self being real when it actually isn't.

Yes, and that can apparently collapse and drop away and may not.

It is going to happen at the apparent physical death anyway. So if I leave here, in the dream, I go out and do whatever gets done, making the prison more comfortable and then death happens – either the death of the body or perhaps when I am tying a shoelace there is suddenly no 'me' – whatever happens it is all good. So I can relax . . .

Who is going to relax? There are teachers who say relax because being separate is fine as it is the expression of wholeness. That is just another idea. For 'me', feeling separate is apparently imprisoning and not at all 'fine'.

But there is nothing that can be done about it?

Does that make you feel better?

In a way there is an anxiety that there is something not

right here anymore, that is missing, that hears this message . . . I don't know what to do with this . . . ?

The belief that you can become free is an illusion. Hope is the thing that keeps 'me' going. All teachings reinforce the sense that one day it will be better; tomorrow will be better. That is not compassion, it is complicity. It is an agreement to reinforce an illusion.

So you would talk about a dream within a dream. Like perception is a dream as well; because nothing really happens and then there is the 'me' arising within the dream.

They are all the same thing. 'Me' is the dream, 'me' is the dreamer and it dreams that it is real and that everything that is happening is real, that is the dream. It is an illusory dream and that is the only illusory dream there is. Everything is just what it is and is not.

There is a way of looking at perception in general, like this whole manifestation is a perception.

'Me' apparently perceives things from a centre that it thinks is real. No 'me', no perceiver. The perception of 'me' the dreamer transforms everything apparently perceived into a solid object, but only to the apparent perceiver. That which is manifest does not need a perceiver . . . it simply is being what is and is not.

So you could say the world exists because of 'me'?

No, not at all! The illusory subject-object world arises only for 'me'. 'Me' wonderfully arrogantly thinks that the world exists because of 'me'. The final result of self-enquiry is that nothing can exist without you, nothing can exist except in your awareness. Because you are aware, things are allowed to be alive. It is unbelievable arrogance. "I am awareness and everything can only arise in that awareness". What 'me' is aware of is an illusory reality only.

We used to believe that the world was flat!

Yes, and also that the Earth was the centre of the Universe; another amazing arrogance! But the 'me' also still believes it is the centre of the human being.

This is curious because you said there was no perception without 'me', so unless there is a 'me' there is no perception. Isn't that what Advaita teachers are saying? And if there is no awareness of this there is nothing?

Again you are not understanding what is being suggested. 'Me' is the perceiver of a dreamt dual reality. When 'me' collapses the perceiver collapses. When there is no illusion of separation there is no perceiver. Whatever arises as something happening is no thing appearing to be a story. Everything, including the world, both is and is not.

The strange part of this is that the suggestion is that when the 'me' falls away, the energy appears as it actually is . . .

It doesn't make an appearance, it simply already is. What then apparently becomes separate from it is 'me'. 'Me' turns it into concrete – within the perception of 'me' only! Everything is apparently only floating particles. That wall is floating particles, it is nothing walling. But then the 'me' perceives everything as a real object.

I get the sense of why this energy is playing this game of seeing and not seeing.

It is hide and seek, God playing hide and seek. The whole thing is a joke. God is a comedian with an audience that never laughs!

Anything you just said you don't know?

There is nothing here that knows anything, it comes out of no thing.

So you have no idea what you are talking about?

If I did you should all leave. There is nothing that can know this. There is nothing to know and nobody to know. It doesn't need to be known. It is an idea that we have to know so that we can control. How can a mystery be controlled?

It comes back to the scientific mind that wants to label everything. Do you think it will ever end?

It won't end because it hasn't begun. It is only the infinite.

There is only what is and isn't.

What is sought remains hidden from the seeker by already being everything.

What seems to be clear is that this message is all or nothing.

Totally, that is all there is . . . everything and no thing.

I feel frustrated. I want to get this but I feel I get it then I don't get it. I can't get to the pivotal point. I want to leave and I want to keep going.

In a way there is always a pivotal point. But you are not getting anywhere because there is nowhere to get to.

There seems to be something automatic going on in the mind. When you are saying things, there is this awful conditioning which believes that everything is happening to me. It is so automatic and it comes and goes.

 That happens in contracted energy . . . apparently.

I keep realising that 'me' has just not heard this, but something draws me to come to this all the time. Although it is constantly blocking out what is being said, at the same time something is happening.

In a way the thing that prompts people to come here is that there is a sense of a personal dilemma. They come and they

73

may find there is nothing personal and there is no dilemma. It can unravel.

I like what you just said – there is no dilemma, we don't have to worry about what to make of all this.

There is nothing to take home and work out.

I feel stunned. There seems to be an intensity of emotions.

'Me' believes it is at the centre of it all.

You said the 'me' was a claiming energy?

Essentially 'me' is an apparently contracted energy which also claims everything. A contracted energy apparently takes form. It gathers everything into itself, it sucks everything in. Thought is only really a report on what apparently did happen or could be happening. The thought that I am separate is only really a verbal report on something much deeper which is energetic. Belief and thought and ideas about being separate are superficial newspaper articles about what is happening. They have no real importance, but 'me' seems to claim them and give them significance.

By itself then the energy of 'me' is useless – it can't even think?

Directly the contraction is formed in the body, there is an identity. Then what arises is the idea that there is someone

74

and that someone then feels that they are managing directors of the story. It is all an illusory and meaningless bit of software.

I get the feeling, listening to you, that you are making 'me' wrong somehow?

Oh, not at all! That would contradict the whole essence of this message which is constantly confirming that everything is fulfilled as it is. The 'me' contraction is only another expression of wholeness . . . it is oneness appearing as two and seeming to be separate. There is no right or wrong, better or worse, but in the separate dreamt experience of the 'me' there seems to be. The open secret is constantly illuminating that illusion.

So it is no good asking who is the 'I', or to whom does this arise. That is just a temporary relaxation?

Anything that is like an investigation seems to be relaxing, because it is a distraction to investigate 'me' and ask 'who am I?' It seems relaxing because it is like an escape.

For energy to start to contract it must have a sense of being in crisis?

The moment of separation is so powerful and so awful, we forget it. There is nothing worse than separating from wholeness. When you are in love with someone and they reject you it is hugely painful. But rejection from wholeness is much more. 'Me' can never remember this. The strange thing is that behind the story there is a sense of something else that is a resonance that something seems lost. There is the belief that one day 'me' will find it again. "Because I am very influential, I can make my life work because I own thoughts and emotions and so I can own enlightenment". It is part of the story to have a teaching that is about 'me' becoming enlightened. But in a way all that the 'me' is trying to do is recompense for that awful loss.

The 'me' searches for peace and fulfilment; the 'me' searches for self-improvement, purity, presence or detachment. The 'me' seeks clarity or any formula which will give the 'me' what it thinks it wants or needs. But the 'me' not getting what it wants is not the dilemma. The dilemma is the apparent 'me'.

But isn't there a sense of pain as well?

The need which goes on and on can never be fulfilled. What is really wanted is actually no thing. It is amazing. People want everything and yet long for no thing. When there is no thing left, there is everything.

Nothing for Sale

The open secret communication can only point to the simple wonder of being, and attempt to illuminate the futility of seeking for it. It does not accept or reject the teachings of spiritual path or process but it will expose, without compromise, the singular and fundamental misconception that drives the belief that there is something called a seeker that needs to find something else called enlightenment.

The open secret does not compromise with the needs and expectations of the seeker. Neither does it attempt to attract or please with promises of an easy and pleasant experience of liberation. Who could promise that and who would experience it?

Because the idea of individual free will and choice is seen as an illusory dream, there is no agenda or intention to help or change individuality. As far as the apparent individual is concerned, there is nothing for sale here.

The sense of being a separate individual feels very real

and affects every part of that apparent experience. It is a state of contracted energy which becomes embodied and which brings with it a feeling of disquiet and longing. There can be a held sense of feeling unworthy and of having lost something indescribable. It is as though the 'me' resides within the boundaries of the body and sees everything outside as something else with which it has to negotiate. Out of these experiences is generated a compulsion to continuously seek comfort or release. This is the dream of individuality which seems real until it doesn't.

The 'me' searches for peace and fulfilment. The 'me' searches for self-improvement or purity, presence or detachment. The 'me' seeks clarity or any formula which will give the 'me' what it thinks it wants or needs. But the 'me' not getting what it wants is not the dilemma. The dilemma is 'me'.

No amount of effort, process, clarity or belief can ever bring anything other than more 'me' searching for that which the 'me' cannot have or know.

The suggestion that separation is only a thought or an understanding that comes or goes in presence is an initially attractive idea for the seeker who dreams of an easy answer which isn't personally challenging and will bring permanent happiness. Thoughts of separation are only individual stories about an already held state of feeling restricted and apart. If separation was only a thought or a belief, it could be seen through or changed to

its opposite, and then 'bingo' there would be liberation . . .
you would think!

Such idealistic communications often go hand in hand
with a relentless reiteration of the idea that separation is
'fine' because there is only ever oneness. This is like telling
a blind person that blindness is 'fine' because all there is is
seeing. Of course there is only oneness. But what apparently
arises in oneness is a deep sense of separation which
doesn't feel 'fine'. These conceptual notions speak only of
symptoms and do not recognise the source of the apparent
dilemma that can fill every part of feeling separate.

In essence what is sought is love. But it is love that is
absolute, all-embracing and eternal. It is this overwhelming
love that many have glimpsed, and which I attempted to
describe in *The Open Secret* when I seemed to be walking
across a park and then was no more. It wasn't experienced
because there was no experiencer. It was a glimpse that
no-one glimpsed. I then returned as 'a someone' and tried
again and again to rediscover that unconditional love which
I would never know.

It is that love which is alluded to in literature, music and
art. The most fascinating love stories are about unrequited
love, because they point to that absolute love which the
individual cannot possess. The powerful fascination of
falling in love comes out of a primal sense that in that love
you could be lost. It is that overwhelming love which is in
all of our longing and is the fullness in the emptiness, the

everything in the nothing. It is unconditional love which also appears as its opposite. Wonderfully, it is also that very love which constantly sings to us through our senses and in every part of the aliveness that is happening.

Liberation is a word used to describe an apparent release from the illusion of feeling imprisoned and apart from love, or wholeness. That shift is essentially an energetic release out of contraction into boundlessness . . . apparently.

Whenever and wherever there is a deep and uncompromising sharing together of the very real paradox of being, a palpable resonance can emerge. Out of that openness there can be a release of that contraction into boundlessness and what arises is the wonder of simply being.

Why is it that the 'me' feels so real?

In a sense that is the whole dilemma of the 'me'. 'Me' as a child grows up into more of a 'me' surrounded by other 'mes' so there is a sense more and more of 'me' being an individual. The main reason is that the whole energy of separation which creates a sense of identity and individuality is a cellular energy held in the body. It is energetic; it is not an idea. You don't grow up with an idea or belief that you are a person; you feel sure that you are an individual in a body.

When I was Tony Parsons I definitely felt as though Tony Parsons lived in this skin and this skin was my boundary. I felt that I was a real person. Growing up, going to school and so on, brings an absolute certainty that you are not only real but that you have free will and choice, you are in your own real story and that cause and effect are real. Increasingly there is a sense of there being a real someone in a world full of other someones. Everything goes on confirming that reality. And out of that comes dissatisfaction born from the experience of being apart from life.

So teachings of enlightenment set out to guide someone along a path or give them a method. These teachings are feeding the whole sense that there is a real person that can take action and do something. That whole sense is once again reinforced by the seeking method. There have been all sorts of paths, like Christianity or Buddhism, a religious path to do with reaching God or heaven.

More recently there have been other teachings that have become more apparent, like self-enquiry. Self-enquiry is a method, a way of developing awareness. Actually 'me' is already living in personal awareness. It is not focused necessarily, but directly the whole energy of 'me' becomes apparent, what comes with it is personal awareness that I exist and that others exist, together with an apparent awareness of the separate world that is out there. It is not focused; it just is personal awareness. It is the way the 'me' takes form and stays separate from being what is, by being aware of it. So 'me' is aware of sitting on a seat. The actual essence of sitting on a seat is kept apart from the 'me'. It is still reinforcing the story of separation. It is called self-consciousness.

Any teaching of this sort simply goes on reinforcing that there is a 'me' that can find something, and self-enquiry is another path towards something fulfilling. It is called enlightenment but actually, through the focusing of awareness, what is really being developed is a sense of detachment. That sense of detachment can seem like enlightenment. Focusing awareness on everything else somehow creates a distance between the knower and life happening. What you apparently build is a sort of ivory tower around 'me' that becomes more and more detached. That feels very freeing for a while. It is closely linked to disassociation.

The great irony is that the self makes the false assumption that it has some uniquely privileged ability to discover something it would call 'ultimate truth' and it expends a lot of energy searching for that. It also believes that it holds some sort of dominion over the rest of creation through its apparent capacity to be aware. However, it is that very awareness that keeps it separate from what it longs for. Everything else, the entire manifestation, is already simply being what the self is trying to grasp.

I agree with what you say about self-enquiry. What about when it is said that hearing happens, thoughts happen and feelings happen? There is no need for a 'me' for things to happen to but there is pure knowing. There is nobody to know it but it happens, but afterwards the 'me' says "I know and I see". Can't this be a pointer and it is just that there is pure knowing?

So called 'pure knowing' is still a function within the whole. If there is a knowing there is a knower. When there is a sense of being separate then one of the things that arises is great fear. One of the ways the fear can be satisfied for a little while is by knowing. If I know what is then I am more in control of it. One of the huge motivations for self-enquiry is for knowing and awareness. Consciousness is a form of knowing and is a way to protect the self from the awful possibility that the self may die and all that will be left is unknowing. That is so frightening for the self that it will create any path that will somehow protect it from that, and then it calls it a spiritual path and this is very satisfying to the higher self which aspires to high ideals.

Progressive teachings of enlightenment which recommend methods such as meditation, self-enquiry, or the idea of acceptance or surrender, are based on the belief in there being a self who can choose to do, or not do, these things. This assumption is invalidated by the recent discovery by neuroscientists that the existence of an individual with free will and choice is illusory.

You said that even if there is not an awareness of the contraction, it is always there?

It comes and goes. In deep sleep it is not there. When the body wakes up usually the whole construct rushes in. There is a whole re-identification of 'me' at the beginning of the day and it is instigated through awareness. However whatever appears doesn't require awareness.

I was wondering what you mean when you say that there is something else happening here, that words are an excuse for something?

There is no thing happening here. In the everything that appears to be happening is the no thing.

So with questions that are asked, are they constantly rejecting the 'me'?

Actually the questions that are asked are trying to support the 'me', trying to find guidance for the 'me', although it can shift from that. There is no one and no thing to give.

Could we just play cards or something?

There is no agenda, there is only what is apparently happening. There is only no thing appearing to be this. It is the same as the shift of energy. Sometimes there is talk about the contracted energy melting back into boundlessness. None of those things are real. They don't actually happen. There is no such thing as real liberation, or real contraction or boundless energy. What there is and isn't can't be described or known, it is this. That is why any idea that you could find it or not is ludicrous. How can you know the unknowable? It is actually in the nature of sitting on a seat or feeling warm. That which is happening is that which can't be known but is constantly longed for.

There is just what is, but sometimes you have said about the appearance . . .

There is only no thing appearing. It is not the absolute and the relative; it is the absolute relative as one thing. There isn't anything else but everything, and that is what is and is not.

The word liberation gives a mind the idea that it can exist and that it can be free?

As far as the seeker is concerned they live in a subject-object reality where the seeker is the subject and enlightenment is the object. So the object of enlightenment feels real . . . that is the dilemma. This is it, it already is. This is it. What is sought, already is; sitting, sounds, breathing, is what is and isn't. All there is is what is happening; thinking is just what is happening. Even the idea that there is a path and a seeker is what is.

Could you say that after liberation everything is the same?

There is no such thing as real liberation. Everything is what it is prior to the end of that which thinks that it is real; in the story of me everything seems real. When the fantasy falls

85

away then it is what it is, without the projection from the 'me' that it isn't. When the 'me' looks at the wall, although the wall is nothing walling, the perception or experience of wall for 'me' is real, solid and apart.

After liberation does neurosis remain?

The brain holds onto trauma and so apparently responds to situations to do with that trauma. After liberation the brain can hold that trauma for a while, but because it cannot find anyone to talk to called 'me' and there is nothing that interacts with it and gives energy to those neuroses, they fall away. But it doesn't matter anyway. The whole thing about 'after liberation' is totally different to the way the seeker thinks about it. Seekers think that the body becomes a perfect vehicle, perfectly moral and accepting and healthy. There are people who appear like that because energy can appear as anything. So there are apparently perfect gurus in the world who fit in with the idea of what personal perfection should look like. It is just a story. Liberation is nothing to do with morality or ethics – they are just simply another way of supporting the story of 'me' and making it feel better and safer for a while.

Can you say something more about nothingness, no thing? Is there such a thing?

All I can say about no thing is that there is an awful lot of it! You are sitting on it, you are breathing it, and this voice is that. There isn't more of no thing and less of everything or the other way round, because one would spill over the side of the cup. There just is nothing and everything simultaneously. It is the paradox.

What are you thinking of right now, you sit there very relaxed?

What is relaxing is that there is nothing here and there is no agenda. Thinking arises but there is no significance because nothing is 'important'. There is no longer anything that relates to 'what is', or is aware of 'what is'. There just is 'what is'. There is nothing moving in and out of anything, there is just 'isness'. So thought is 'isness', sitting on a seat is 'isness'. There is simply 'being', but even that word isn't it.

In the last hour the sensations are gone and something is appearing but there is really no thing, and then I think I have come back. It is difficult.

All the time there is a 'me' there is no way this can be recognised. It is only absolutely obvious when there is no one. The 'me' thinks this is ridiculous, but when the 'me' collapses it is absolutely ridiculous that there could be a 'me'. It is so obvious, but when this happens to people, they cannot explain it. That is how it remains hidden from the seeker, by being everything, and so the seeker can't find it because it is looking for a something that it can know in everything.

You are saying that nothing can bring forth this liberation and yet you are saying that it is liberating to sit in this energy. You could say there is nothing to gain because we are all the same oneness – so why is it liberating to be in this energy?

It is liberating for no-one and so there is nothing to gain. The apparent liberation is from the apparently contracted experience. But it is a story. There is no one here that can choose to be here or not. It has nothing to do with anyone being anywhere because all there is is boundlessness.

Did you go through a religious phase? How do you look on mankind – did God have an off day when he created mankind?

Actually it was mankind that created God. The idea of God creating mankind only arises in the dream of 'me'. All there is is energy, wholeness, there is nothing running that. It has no direction, it is chaotic and ordered. It is no thing arising as energy, apparently happening. It has no purpose or meaning at all. There is no meeting between this and any sort of religious or spiritual teaching. This is not a personal teaching, it is completely non-prescriptive. It suggests something. It has no agenda or intention, and there is nothing available. It is the wonderful message of hopelessness, which is unconditional love and the only compassion.

I get a picture in my head of invisible lamps and energy floating around the room. Then I open my eyes and I see human beings with hair and clothes. Is that closer to the reality?

As far as the 'me' is concerned it doesn't see the natural reality, it sees an artificial reality. The 'me' sees an apparent something else arising, like people. It is that which is not two appearing to be a dualistic reality.

But energy is invisible?

No it isn't, you are looking at it, energy is everything. If there is a 'me' it doesn't see energy, it sees a fixed solid thing which it thinks is another object. When there is no 'me' it is obvious all is just energy. In reality you are moving particles which come together to form that. No will, no purpose and no meaning, just what is and is not.

Is your expression coming from that energy?

No, I don't have an expression. There is nothing left; all there is, is what is. This response is coming from no thing and that question is coming from no thing.

Does the energy take on this form?

It doesn't take it on. It is already no thing appearing as everything. The energy is both real and unreal, it just is. It is timeless, it just is. There is no before and after, and this isn't going to continue because it didn't begin. It is as it is and is not.

It seems that everything is so chaotic and suddenly I saw it from the other way. When I am there it has to be ordered in a certain way. When it is just chaotic it is a miracle that there is a voice or a body.

The meaning of chaotic is that it is unpredictable and unknowable. The 'me' thinks it knows this and has sorted it all. This is a room, these are people and I am a person, so it is all alright. The 'me' thinks it knows things and knowing them makes it safe. It creates an artificial world to escape reality because it is scared. The reality is that what is, is wild and free. It is the desperate desire of the 'me' to know itself, the idea of consciousness knowing itself and thereafter being in control is the goal.

The final, ultimate result promised with many teachings is that the reward of meditation or self-enquiry is the sudden knowing of consciousness as the final liberation. The 'me' is so desperate to be in control that even its idea about enlightenment is still about the higher 'me' knowing something. It is still safe. The ultimate obsession of the 'me' is to know, it thinks it has to know. It believes it has to be in something called 'present knowing'.

So, because this is completely unknowable there is nothing you can get hold of here. Don't bother to try and get hold of some idea to take home with you. There is nothing here that is of any use to the seeker at all. There is nothing for sale. You can't get this right or wrong. You can't go away from this or move nearer to it. You can't act in a certain way that makes this right. You can't try and look for no 'me'. So there is no point in trying to be no 'me', or trying to get hold of this or that idea.

What is wonderful about this is that wherever you go and whatever you do, what you long for never leaves. It constantly is all there is.

What is boredom and who feels boredom?

Boredom is the seeking 'me' looking for something to excite itself so that it can feel alive. That is why there is currently such a fascination with emotions. Everything has to be more and more emotional nowadays so that we don't get bored. It is the dilemma of the 'me' – rushing round in a circle looking for the next event. The 'me' lives in what will be and cannot possibly recognise what is.

Does physical pain change with the 'not me'?

Pain is nothing 'paining'. If 'me' is there it takes ownership of the pain and calls it its own – my pain – I am in pain. When there is 'no me' then there is just pain. When there is a 'me' it turns it into a story – me and my pain – it turns it into a drama. Pain is pain, walls are walls and cars are cars – there is only 'what is', apparently.

Is there any quality like openness, sincerity or honesty that can be helpful?

The 'me' wants to get an idea about how it could be, like sincere. The 'me' can't be open; it daren't be open. The 'me' is always locked in the journey. The 'me' adopts virtues in the story but they have no value in the whole. There is no need for the 'me' to have virtue; it doesn't matter if you are grossly dishonest – this would happen regardless of that, there is no interest in what you are like . . . there is no you to be 'like' anything.

Life is not a task. There is absolutely nothing to attain except the realisation that there is absolutely nothing to attain.

Whatever is beyond, or oneness, is it looking through these eyes so is it looking at itself?

No, anything looking is still in the story – there isn't anything here looking, there is only what there is. This is unknowable, we are sharing a mystery here. What is being described will not make sense. The 'me' can think that it is looking or observing, but that is a function. There is no subject and no object.

. . . and doing?

Every word should have 'apparent' before it. There is the appearance of doing – this is an appearance of a room with bodies in it who apparently do things – it is simply wholeness appearing as this. There is no such thing as an individual who does things; they appear to do them. It is the most exquisite, wondrous game.

So is there nothing like seeing, a kind of recognition of it?

Initially at the point of liberation, or death of the body, there is an impersonal recognition that there never was anyone or anything to become liberated. Liberation is the end of something that was never happening. There only is what is and thereafter there isn't something walking round with this recognition. It seems as though there is something here describing it, or knowing that there is only what is, but there isn't. That is the paradox of communicating like this; there only is what is, and it can't be described.

After liberation has the contracted sense of self gone?

You are telling a story. It was never there, so it hasn't gone. It was never really there to go away. It would appear in the wholeness as a sense of separation. But when that which never was happening is no more then there is nothing to return to.

Are you standing there experiencing 'what is'? Can you make the difference between standing before and after liberation? Is there a difference between sitting and looking at the wall for instance?

93

No, there is just 'what is'. There is no 'me' standing here. 'What is' cannot be described. It is unknowable. All that can be said is that standing is what is and that is timeless. It is the infinite expression. This is no thing appearing to happen. Standing is the natural reality.

So the 'me' is addicted to the 'me'. So what is no thing?

Out of no thing arises the story of 'me' which is addicted to itself. 'Me' seeking is the absolute expression of wholeness, the absolute appearing as this. It is uniquely human and nothing else has the sense of a separate identity. No thing is no thing and it cannot be known. Out of no thing arises awareness, seeking, motor cars, and marmalade! No thing is everything, emptiness is fullness.

I can relate to what you are saying, words like indescribable, unknowable. But when you talk about 'no thing' standing, I get confused.

But it is the same thing. It is a mystery. It is amazing. How can there be and not be something? It can't be recognised by 'me' because 'me' believes that this is real and only real . . . when that collapses it is suddenly absolutely obvious that it is no thing appearing as that. It is a mystery for the 'me' which cannot comprehend it. When there is no 'me' it is obvious, and it is freedom.

When the assumed sense of being separate seems to collapse, already there is only the constant and unknowable wonder of being.

It seems odd to speak about it, as language is all about 'me'; so how do you talk about a totally different reality?

The natural reality is beyond the speaking of it. However the difference with what is being communicated here and elsewhere is that it is simply pointing to the infinite, it doesn't point away from the infinite like a teaching. The infinite can't be found, can't be taught or understood. In a sense the words are useless but they too are no thing 'wording'. So they have an energy. What is essentially going on here is energetic and beyond words.

I have a question about the meaning of the word 'is'?

The best expression is 'all there is' is 'what is and isn't'. Nobody understands it. There is no one here who would need to understand it because it is obvious that 'all there is' is 'what is and isn't' – both together at the same time. It is a mystery.

It is so strange that we kind of know this is meaningless. The 'me' creates all these disturbances and still we maintain it?

The 'story of me' is fascinating and also the 'me' is fascinated by the idea that it is going to find fulfilment.

So it has to be a total dissolving of the 'me' to get this and give up?

Yes, but 'me' can't do that. It is the disillusionment.

So if 'me' can't get it, does it just disappear or give up?

The 'me' can't dissolve itself. The 'me' can't give up because the 'me' is the story of separation and the seeking of oneness.

So sensing what is as an object is another form of the 'me' in the story?

Yes, it is still the story. Sensing 'what is' is like being aware of what is. There has to be something apart to be aware. The nearest you can say is that which is apart from 'what is' is suddenly eaten by what is. Then that is the end. 'Me' is eaten and dies in 'what is'.

Somehow it doesn't seem so scary any more.

No, it is not at all scary, but it is for 'me'. It is very simple and ordinary but all the time there is a 'me' there it is scary because it is about dying. 'Me' doesn't know what it is longing for so the death of 'me' is unknown to 'me'. 'Me' is knowing or awareness so it is very frightened about stopping knowing. When there is an opening to this 'me' can begin to fall apart, or crumble or lessen its strength, and when that happens 'me' will fight for itself or not be so scared of not being there. Then waking up can happen one morning and there is no 'me' there. You don't have to go through some drama about this, it is very ordinary.

Is it possible that there are some teachers and their 'me' has collapsed, but they are just going along with the illusion?

When the 'me' apparently collapses there is no one to teach and no one to learn. Supporting the illusion of separation by teaching a path is not compassion; it is a complicity to support illusion. It is also what is and isn't.

You seem to attack teachers and teachings quite a lot. Why is that?

Firstly teachers as such have never been personally attacked because it is recognised that the 'I', 'self' or 'me' is an illusion. However a teaching of becoming which, from the open secret perspective, keeps the seeker locked into that illusion will be constantly exposed . . .

Why is it that now there are so many different sorts of therapies and teachings which claim to be non-dual?

The term non-dual has been plagiarised in an attempt to satisfy the seeker's beliefs and hopes that there is a something called non-duality that can be attained through personal choice and effort. A good example of this is a claim by self-enquiry teachers that if the 'I' believes that it can choose between being 'embroiled' in separation or, given sufficient courage, honesty and humility, not be 'embroiled' in separation, then it is granted a special concession to choose one or the other.

It has to be assumed that this special concession is granted by 'God', or the modern equivalent 'Consciousness', to those few who are considered worthy of such a privilege. It is puzzling that such a pseudo-religious fantasy like this could be seen as having any kind of connection with the essence of non-duality. However, the apparent 'I' can be very clever and determined to survive.

What about conditioning in some traditions?

That would be 'me' being conditioned into believing that there is a tradition and a traditional teaching. This is based on the confirmation that 'me' is real and that it can choose to move from A to B. This is born out of the dualistic belief that the so-called absolute is separate from the so-called relative, and that the seeker needs to rise from the lowly relative into the lofty absolute. This false assumption is at the foundation of all teachings of becoming as described in the last answer.

Isn't it ok if it works?

There you go again, dreaming. The 'me' dreams that something can work; that there will be a result. It is the whole root of teaching and seeking. No thing doesn't need anything to work; the whole principle of all teaching is to make something work, to make it change. But why would no thing, which is everything, want to change anything when everything is completely fulfilled already. Why would the infinite want to make something better?

Doctrines, processes and progressive paths which seek enlightenment only exacerbate the problem they address by reinforcing the idea that the self can find something that it presumes it has lost. It is that very effort, that investment in self-identity, that continuously recreates the illusion of separation from oneness. It is the dream of individuality.

What about emotions and what about actions that follow on from that?

Emotions are energy in an apparent form. They are 'what is', as are actions. When the 'me' collapses then there is just that, apparently. Anger happens and yes, there can be actions or not – but only apparently. The only way of describing this is that all there is is what happens, apparently.

There are some places that people say have special influences, is that so?

It is a dream that is about subject-object worlds and there being some places that are different; it has nothing to do with this message. The problem for 'me' is that it is looking for something significant like a holy mountain or someone who seems to be holy, or quiet or spiritual. It is pure dualism and also it is what is and isn't.

But a mountain can have an energy, so . . . ?

There is only energy, so this mountain can have this energy and another mountain another energy; both are appearances of wholeness without significance of any kind. The 'me' is just constantly looking for a sign or an answer; there isn't one. There can't be an answer because there isn't any question. If there was a question or an answer there would be somewhere to get to and something to have and know.

How can this be ordinary and be love? How can there be frustration and pain, then wonder, and that be love?

Unconditional love is everything; frustration, anger, pain, joy . . . all those things. It is absolute wholeness and it can't be comprehended. It is all inclusive and that is why what you long for never leaves you. It is constantly there in the frustration, the joy, whatever. All of that is the beloved.

Life is its own purpose and doesn't need a reason to be. That is its beauty.

The contraction of energy in the body, is it only human, is that the 'me'?

The idea of 'me' happens but it is not a thought or a belief, it is energetic. The idea 'I am me' is just information, a confirmation, and means nothing. If you change the thought to 'I am everything' it is just information in the head.

Could it not be a terminological issue? Buddha calls it the no self.

All these are ideas that teachings have to give the seeker an answer; finding the no self! It is just offering somebody something they dream they can have. You can't put this into language. Having said that there are two forms of language; one form points to the infinite and the other points away from it. That which is a personal teaching is a language that points away from the infinite because it is telling you that you can find it. This communication only uses a language which points to the infinite but doesn't suggest it can be defined or known.

From wherever and whenever this insight is communicated, it has no connection with end-gaining, belief, path or process. It cannot be taught but is constantly shared. Because it is all that is, no-one can lay claim to it. It needs not to be argued, proven or embellished, for it stands alone simply as it is, and can only remain unrecognised and rejected, or realised and lived.

What is what is?

All there is is what is . . . but what is what is?

Well, there is no real answer to that question. However, it seems that what is could be just what is happening. . . reading these words, sitting on a seat, trees growing, sounds, feelings, clouds or thoughts passing by and so on. In simple terms these events just seem to be what is happening. But the perspective here is that the essence of what is happening is an open secret.

It is suggested that what is is oneness appearing as twoness, the absolute being relative. It is the treasure that is longed for and feared most . . . the perfect lover and the grim reaper. It is of course the ultimate paradox, being simultaneously nothing and everything.

There is no possibility of the essence of 'what is' being described, grasped or known. The seeker attempts to be aware of or conscious of what is and immediately that function separates and objectifies and makes solid that which is wonderfully floating, effervescent and ungraspable.

The essence of what is can't be seen by 'me' and so 'me' never feels fulfilled because its experiences seem to have something missing.

In what is is also what isn't. This is the wonder of wholeness because it appears as both simultaneously. Everything that is something is also already no thing . . . there are not two! Everything is therefore real and unreal, but 'me' experiences everything as only real. Within this illusion 'me' attempts to transform this dualistic and unsatisfactory experience into processes such as 'living in the moment' or 'being here now' or accepting everything as 'consciousness'. However, these are all only inconstant experiences seeking the only unobtainable constant . . . everything.

However, and again the wonderful paradox of the play of wholeness is, that the story of 'me' is also what is. All of the dreams and hopes, processes and religious aspirations are only wholeness appearing as a separate entity rushing around looking for itself and also hiding from itself by already being everything. And in being everything, even the avoidance or rejection of what is, is what is.

So what is longed for constantly sings the only song of freedom that can never be lost or found because it is already all there is.

What we are sharing is an exposure of the artificial construct of the 'me' that is always looking for something more to satisfy itself – always living in what will be. In that illumination the possibility can arise that the construct of the 'me' can collapse. It is inconstant, it comes and goes and it has no reality. It is not the words that make this happen; clarity and understanding is not liberation. The collapse of the 'me' is essentially energetic. 'Me' is an apparent energy that is held; it is a constrained energy. When the feeling of separation arises, directly afterwards there is fear and a tension, a sense of trying to hold this together and control it. That whole construct is artificial and suddenly it can just collapse. That is the end of the story, and all that is left is life happening. When there is nothing left of the 'me' it cannot be described and it is impossible for the 'me' to comprehend what it is like not to be there. There is simply what is and is not.

Driving down the motorway just now coming here, I was thinking, "I am not here". So driving when liberated would happen, but you know you are not doing it?

No, you don't sit in a car knowing you are not there anymore. Liberation isn't knowing there is no 'me'. What we are talking about is the death, the end of something that isn't real, which is the separate identity. So there isn't something that knows it isn't there, or anything that knows it is at one, there is just driving a car. Nobody does it, there is just natural functioning – it doesn't need me. Neuroscientists have discovered that the brain constructs the 'me'. Driving a car happens. That whole judgement about how I should be driving isn't there anymore.

So it isn't a shift of perspective from 'me' to a 'no me'?

No, it isn't a shift of perspective. You could only describe it as the apparent end of an illusion that was never real. But even that doesn't happen. It is as though there is a constrained energy which suddenly frees up. If you want to describe it as something that happens, that is the nearest you can get to it. However, a recognition arises, for no one, that there never was a constrained energy.

You mentioned that it was a process happening to the body.

It is an apparent energetic shift from being a constrained centre back into the natural reality which is that there is only everything. But it doesn't happen to a person.

I woke up one night and there was no one there. It was very distressing and uncomfortable and I had to get out of bed. It was terrifying.

It varies a lot; it can be terrifying and also cool.

If it is indescribable, how has it ever been communicated? What is it? There is no shift, no change, so how is it possible to communicate it?

It can't be described or communicated. All that is happening here is the exposure that surrounds the myth of identity. The communication here is about that, and there is no way it can describe freedom. It is unknowable.

It is so obvious and simple, any attempt to grasp it obscures it. Never found, never knowable, being is the consummate absence that is beyond measure.

So there is no 'how'?

No, this is not a personal teaching; there is no 'how'. The 'me' fears and longs for its own absence.

So what is going on here?

Apparently nothing. This is a meeting which, for the individual, is absolutely pointless. There is nothing here for the individual at all. The seeking energy is starved.

So how did the 'I/me' come to make such a big mistake?

Nobody made a mistake. Energy just appeared as an individual. Nobody did it. The 'I' feels as if it has lost something and therefore, now that it is an identity, there must be something wrong with it. So then the 'I' goes to find out what is wrong with it and tries to learn how to be better. It is a completely futile activity based on a false assumption.

I understand it but I still want to seek.

The 'I' is the seeking. It is futile but it can only seek because
it is constantly aware and therefore separate. In some way or
other, when the absolute dilemma is exposed, there can be a
recognition of the ridiculousness of it all. Then there can be
an 'aahh!' and possibly something can collapse, apparently.

Can the fear stop it happening?

'Me' tries everything to stop it happening. 'Me' naturally
rejects this message because it means that 'me' would
die. Nothing can stop it happening because it doesn't
happen. When suddenly 'me' collapses there is an instant
recognition, by no one, that there never was anyone or
anything to collapse. There can be a lot of fear because it is
apparently impersonal. 'Me' wants to know it is ok.

*You say that people can't describe it when it happens – isn't
that isolating for you?*

It is the very opposite. It is the ultimate love affair. There is
only the beloved so who is there to be isolated? It is beyond
intimacy. What is is everything. It doesn't need a knower.
That which knows the wind is blowing, is isolated from the
wind blowing. How can unconditional love be isolated?

*Awareness is what is as well. So if there is no 'me' what is
responding?*

108

There is only what is, including awareness. Awareness and knowing are functions which maintain apparent separation. When 'me' collapses so does awareness. Awareness is knowing, and to know something you need to be apart from it. It only happens in the dualistic dream in a subject-object reality. When 'me' collapses there is nothing that knows what is. Response is energy responding . . . apparently.

to be a subject you need to fix objects in place

So it seems that the 'me' always seeks to put a reason on everything. When 'me' is gone there is just fear, love . . .

'Me' believes falsely that it has to know, to be in control. It has to know why it is afraid so that it can deal with it. All there is is what is and is not.

Ultimately it is an apparent unfolding of no thing. No thing is appearing to be a person who knows and is in control. For the 'me' it is all really important to make its artificial reality better. The difference with a meeting like this is that there is no recognition that anything has any fixed reality. There is only what is and isn't. 'Me' plays games and takes on a role. All of that completely collapses, so there is nothing here that is self-conscious and there aren't any games. The complicity ends. The only compassion is to expose that which apparently imprisons. There is nothing wrong or right with anything, it is just what is happening.

So there is nothing you can take away from these meetings . . . no personal teaching, no formulas, no processes or beliefs. You can't 'do' or 'not do' what is communicated here. Also you can't get it right or wrong. There simply is only what is and is not . . . that's it. And wherever you go and whatever you do, think or feel, that is what is.

It is the only constant that never comes and never goes away. It is the perfect lover . . . it is the abiding song of love that is nothing and everything.

Thank you.

Meetings and residentials with Tony Parsons take place regularly in the UK and internationally.

For details of the above and how to contact Tony, visit the website at:
www.theopensecret.com

Lightning Source UK Ltd.
Milton Keynes UK
UKOW01f0715130416

272136UK00001B/25/P